Cihacek

# Heloise's
# Hints
# for
# Working
# Women

# Heloise's Hints for Working Women

PRENTICE-HALL, Inc., Englewood Cliffs, N. J.

*Frontispiece by Dale Randall*

*Illustrations by Frank Fletcher*

HELOISE'S HINTS FOR WORKING WOMEN
by Heloise

Copyright © 1970, 1969, 1968, 1967, 1966, King
Features Syndicate, Inc.

ISBN–0–13–386383–2

Library of Congress Catalog Card Number:
75–101011

Printed in the United States of America   T

Prentice-Hall International, Inc., London
Prentice-Hall of Australia, Pty. Ltd., Sydney
Prentice-Hall of Canada, Ltd., Toronto
Prentice-Hall of India Private Ltd., New Delhi
Prentice-Hall of Japan, Inc., Tokyo

*This book was written with a bushel of love
and a bucket full of kisses for you—
the precious working gal.*

Love,

Heloise

*Other books by the author*

*Heloise's Housekeeping Hints*
*Heloise's Kitchen Hints*
*Heloise All Around the House*
*Heloise's Work and Money Savers*

# Contents

# Heloise's Hints for Working Women

# Preface

This book was written to you from my heart and soul —and to you alone, not your friends, kinfolks, or in-laws— but *you*, the working gal! In grandmother's day, a housewife spent *all* her time in her home. But today it is no longer necessary for you gals to be chained to your home.

For one thing, as those of you who have read my other books and my columns know, there are millions of shortcuts to help the busy housewife and working woman get her work done in far less time. And take it from me, any hint or trick or shortcut that will make that housework easier is worth giving a try.

It is entirely possible to run a satisfactory house, keep that hubby and the kiddies happy, and still have time for whatever outside interest you choose. It's a *wonderful* world and just full of *wonderful* things to do, and you, dear gal, deserve to do them.

1

If you decide to go back to work—answer me this—who'll complain? I'm sure that those little extras you provide will be appreciated by your hard-working husband and children. What a lift it will give you to be able to afford a few special luxuries every once in awhile. And because you are happy and a joy to live with, your family will appreciate you even more.

If it's charity work that you're just dying to get your fingers into—go ahead and do it. Your family couldn't help but be proud of you for devoting some of your time and talents to others.

But the most important point that I want to make is—whether it's working in an office, teaching, nursing, doing volunteer work with the Red Cross or the Cub Scouts—go to it, gal, and don't feel guilty—not even for *one minute*.

Your home and family won't suffer. This book is for you, and you'll find hints for on the job and off, for making your housekeeping tasks lighter, thus giving you more time for yourself.

First of all, never try to keep a perfect home. There is no such thing as perfection. Why try to achieve it? When you look around your home and see so many things that need to be done, always remember what Heloise told you —"other people do not see all these things."

Never work when you are overtired. Just tell the family that "Mother is tired." After all, you work as hard (or harder) than anyone else. And if you ever want an *excuse* for the way you do your work, just say "Heloise said so!" And blame it all on me.

Instead of cleaning the whole house with a vengeance every six months, why not clean one room thoroughly when the mood strikes you and let the rest of the house "glide." This way you never really get behind.

Pick up the big chunks daily—either before work or after—and get the middle clean. This will inspire you to eventually getting around to thorough cleaning. At least once a week use your very best Sunday dishes and silver. Serve the meal at the dining room table. You'll be surprised how much better the same food will taste and how your family will love it. They'll feel that they are getting extra-special attention and are still Mom's first love, even though she does work.

Remember life is so short, so let's live it to the fullest. Time is the one thing we cannot buy or recapture. Just look, it has taken you at least a few minutes to read this. And those minutes are gone. Don't work yourself to death, but keep in mind that *the second wife always has a maid* . . .

Heart attacks and nervous breakdowns aren't too hard to come by, so say many psychiatrists. Besides the doctor bills, tranquilizers are expensive (and it is a proven fact that we can't live on them forever), so brace your back, hold your chin up, get that smile on your face, and let's do the best we can.

Housewives are the backbone of America, so why don't you spoil yourselves just a little?

I give you my heart—and love you always.

Heloise

# Chapter 1

# ❦ Mini-Homemaking

Taking care of your home sometimes seems like *more* than a full-time job, but most of us nowadays simply aren't around full time. Most of us have other jobs (at least part-time ones), and some of us are nine-to-fivers, desperately in need of all the shortcuts in existence (and some that aren't!) for getting our daily housekeeping chores done.

## ❦ *Laundry*

If you're working, a good part of your evenings and weekends should be time for family and fun. Believe me, you've earned it, honey! You need some tricks to make your laundry, ironing, mending, and baking a breeze.

One way is to share the load! For instance, say you just hate doing the wash. Well, someday when you're talking with your neighbors or kinsfolk (especially those who also

5

have outside jobs) tell them how you feel. They'll probably come right back with, "And I despise ironing!"

Right *then* is the time to say, "Well, you bring your laundry over to my house, and I'll do all of your ironing while you do my washing. How about that?"

This actually did work recently with two neighbors and myself. What's more, they brought along their kids, their peanut butter sandwiches, and their own jars of instant coffee. It got to where the three of us enjoyed Laundry Day.

While the washing machine was going, I sewed on the ripped-off buttons. Then it got down to where each of us brought our own packages of hamburger. We cooked spaghetti sauce all day and divided it in thirds!

Later on, we met at each other's homes every third week. That was a relief, too, to get out of our own homes.

Once I took my portable sewing machine and mended all of their clothes while they did both my washing and ironing. They didn't even know how to sew or take up hems, much less run a sewing machine.

Love is where you find it, and it's even greater yet if you can share it. So pack up your troubles in your old laundry bag and when you find a good friend like this, take your iron and clothes over to her house. All of you will learn to get the laundry done in short order and with pleasure.

## ✵ Washer Woes

Face it, gals—those clothes just have to be washed eventually, and you might as well do the job right. A word of advice on laundering wash-and-wear clothing in your washing machine: *Don't,* please don't, try to do as big a machine load of wash-and-wears as you would of other items, such as sheets and towels. It's far better to do only half as large a load. This prevents crowding, and there is less chance of setting wrinkles in the garments. And *never* use hot water. Use either cold or lukewarm.

Another good tip on wash-and-wearables:

"I use a skirt hanger that holds six garments for drying my drip-drys.

"I hang it over the bathtub on the shower nozzle and close the shower curtain, so the bathroom will look neat.

"Sure fools my friends!"

I'm sure all you clever working gals buy whatever you can that's wash-and-wear, permanent press, and so on. (The less ironing the better!) Many of you have asked about caring for the permanent press garments. Here's some information I received recently from the United States Department of Agriculture:

"These garments carry 'no iron' labels and it is important to know how to take care of them.

"Avoid getting fabric very soiled. Some synthetic fibers used in durable press items absorb and hold on to oily soil, thus it's best to wash often and avoid soil buildup.

"Pretreat heavily soiled areas or grease spots by rubbing in a detergent paste or liquid detergent before washing. Test first on an inconspicuous area and make sure that all items treated this way resist fading. If color is fast, let the detergent remain on the fabric for 10 to 15 minutes.

On color-sensitive fabrics, remove greasy soil with a dry-cleaning solution, then wash by hand with a mild soap or detergent. Wash and rinse quickly, roll loosely in a towel and hang to dry.

"Wash in small loads and use the right laundry products. Bleaching yellows some fabrics. Read and follow manufacturer's directions. Fabric softeners reduce static electricity, make garments feel softer, and often help prevent wrinkling.

"Warm or cool water and short wash, rinse and spin cycles are important. The heat and tumbling action of an automatic dryer relaxes fibers and removes wrinkles that occur during wearing and washing. Turn the heat off for the last 10 minutes of the drying cycle. As soon as the tumbling stops, remove and hang garments and curtains."

### Corduroy

"As a manufacturer of corduroy, I would like to offer a few tips on how to wash this material.

"We always suggest that you turn the garment inside out before washing or drying it!

"This way it can be washed either by machine or by hand. Because in the washing process you are buffing the naps against each other which makes for cleaner corduroy.

"If it must be pressed, always press on the wrong side. We recommend using a steam iron. This must be done lightly and quickly. And the reason is that the nap should not collect too much steam.

"Another tip is if any corduroy garment has a lining, dry cleaning is recommended—either professional or by coin-operated dry-cleaning machines.

"The reason for this is that manufacturers of corduroy do not know what kind of lining is used. Sometimes the lining in garments will shrink (especially if it's an inexpensive cotton)."

Here's another tip that really works:
"To remove lint from dark corduroy:
"Wash and allow to dry slowly, and while the article still is slightly damp, just brush it with a clothes brush. All of the lint will come off.
"This works like magic every time.
"It is very important that the clothing be damp when trying to remove the lint because lint really sticks after corduroy is dry."
Better yet—use nylon net!

### Midnight Laundress
This working gal has a terrific idea:
"Since I have an office job during the day, I do most of my housework in the evening.
"I have only one clothesline and no dryer, so I have a little plan which I call 'getting an early start.'
"I hang several small items such as handkerchiefs, socks, underwear, dish and wash cloths, etc., on a clothes hanger, using a clothespin on each item. In fact, I hang everything on hangers, using clothespins on the items that might fall off.
"I hang all these filled hangers on a rod in the shower overnight, and in the morning before I leave for work, I just take the hangers outside and pin them to the line with clothespins. It saves space and the hangers of dry clothes are easy to collect.
"If the weather is bad, I leave the clothes-laden hangers on the shower curtain rod, turn on the bathroom heater, and close the door."

Dime store chalk is excellent to remove body oil stains and lines along the neck of washable blouses and shirts. Just draw the white line over the soiled places and put them in your hamper for a few days. On laundry day the chalk has absorbed the oil and soil washes out easily.

The same works on grease spots, and on nice white table linens too. Rub the chalk on both sides of the grease spot. Some people use talcum powder or cornstarch.

Others immediately find a cake of dry white soap and rub the spot, and a little area around it, then wash.

On men's soiled shirt collar lines, many wives say they use shampoo! Yes, the same stuff they wash their hair with.

If you use a boxed powder form, when doing laundry or dishes . . . Don't *ever* throw away that empty box until you pour some warm water in it, shake and pour out again. You'll get enough out of it for another job. More pennies saved.

Always wash and dry dark slacks or pants *wrong* side out to prevent them from collecting lint.

If you use spray starch on dark clothes, spray on the *wrong* side of the material, and there will be no chance of starch marks.

Any time your washing machine overflows from just-too-much suds, don't scream. Just grab that box of salt and sprinkle away! Excess suds will vanish like magic.

Turn men's and boys' pants wrong side out before putting them in the dryer. The pockets dry much faster, whereas they usually are the last part of the pants to get dry.

Keep a small squeeze bottle filled with liquid laundry detergent beside your washing machine.

When collars and cuffs need to be scrubbed, just squirt some detergent in the proper place, rub it in a little, and then place in the machine.

And one fellow used to be in the laundry business, and here is a little hint he passed along to women who cannot get the soiled line out of their husband's shirt collars.

They removed these by rubbing a little ammonia on the collars before putting them in the washing machine. They particularly liked the sudsy kind. They did not find that it damaged the material or caused fading.

It also helps prevent this line on shirt collars if men will pour some rubbing alcohol on a washcloth and rub their neck with it every so often (their own neck, not the shirt's!).

Another sweetheart wrote:

"When I forget to take a no-iron item from the dryer and it has stayed there long enough to accumulate wrinkles, all I do is put in some wet laundry. Then I let the no-iron item go through the tumbling process along with the wet clothes.

"The steam from the wet items smooths out the wrinkles in the no-iron garment. As soon as the dryer stops, I put it on a clothes hanger to preserve the smooth finish."

We busy housewives often forget to remove clothes from the dryer as soon as it stops. We have been told to put damp bath towels in it. This way you have an extra amount of moisture, and the weight of the wet towels hits the no-iron item and helps take out those unwanted wrinkles.

*Never overdry no-irons*, and always remember them the instant your machine stops.

## ❦ Iron Easy

Do you know how many hours the average woman spends at her ironing board?

Add up your weekly hours and multiply them by the 52 weeks in each year, times the number of years you expect to live! You'll be amazed.

If you don't have an adjustable ironing board, why don't you run out, not walk, and buy one? Or borrow or rent one from your neighbor, and try it out. Once you have used an adjustable board, you won't be without one.

Common sense tells us it's easier to iron a garment while sitting down—with the iron below waistline height. This takes far less energy (energy that you working gals need) than reaching up when sitting at a too-high ironing board, or standing up to iron.

If we spend five or ten dollars on a good adjustable ironing board, there's no reason to feel guilty. Think of the hours we spend ironing.

And did you know, that if you would put a couple of layers of foil under your ironing board cover, it would reflect the heat and your ironing would go faster?

For those of you tempted to talk away your ironing time, here's a good solution:

"Telephone conversations can liven any dreary day. But they can also cause loss of precious time, particularly on ironing day.

"Set up your ironing board by the phone and have a clear conscience while gabbing with those long-winded— but much loved—friends and relatives. Just buy and attach one of those gadgets to hold your phone on your shoulder while you talk.

"Incidentally, there's no better place for your mending

basket either than beside the phone for use during those unexpected long calls."

That's a surefire way to get your work done! Now, if we could figure out a way to set up the coffee makings there too, wouldn't that be great?

When you get that new ironing board cover, iron on a dab of paraffin (old white candle wax will do) into the wide end of it.

If your iron starts sticking, just run it over the waxed part, and it will glide along smooth as silk. Some people fold waxed paper a few times and use this.

Others wrap a piece of old white candle in a few folds of an old T shirt or bath towel, and wipe it over the iron from time to time. It's great.

A good quick easy way to iron blue jeans is to put them on pant stretchers and *then* iron away. Personally, I can't imagine why anyone should ever waste time ironing blue jeans.

Fold 'em at the knee and commence rolling them from the knee up towards the belt line, and put them away in that roll.

And did you know that the manufacturers write me: "The crease is not supposed to be in the front, but along the side as they are folded when they come from the factory."

Do you have to wear gloves to work? Want to know how to press the white cotton ones? My answer is, don't.

After washing gloves in a mild detergent, the best thing to do is to hold them under your hot water faucet and let the water run into them. This only takes a few seconds. When they are thoroughly rinsed by that nice hot water —and remember, your thermostat should be set at least at 140°—hold them up by the cuff with your fingertips until the water drips out.

Then when the glove cools enough, hold it by the cuff and slap it against the bathroom mirror, with the thumb side towards you. With your hand, rub the glove so that it is pressed and sticks to the mirror. Then all you have to do is leave it alone to dry.

They won't fall off until they are completely dry. And if they are heavy, they won't even then.

They will look as good as the day you bought them.

Gals, this is the only way I know to make a glove look like new.

Another good idea on the subject of white gloves: After you take your gloves off the mirror, spray the palm sides and the fingertips with starch and then let it dry. The starch will keep the cotton from absorbing the soil and prevents a lot of scrubbing later.

### Pleats and Hems

"Since I do alterations, I have to press a lot of hems and cuffs. I've learned a way to do this without putting a shine on the cloth.

"I put a piece of heavy brown paper bag over the material, moisten the top of the paper with a damp cloth and then iron. It leaves a nice press with no shine whatsoever.

"This works well with all types of materials, especially wool, and is excellent for trousers."

"I have a number of wool pleated skirts that need pressing between cleanings.

"After struggling for ages to keep the pleats in place on the ironing board (with no success), I came up with the idea of using a terry cloth towel on the board under the skirt.

"Now I can iron two or three pleats at a time instead of one, because the wool clings to the towel."

### Shortcut

From a hubby worth his weight in gold: "I just saw my wife put water into her steam iron. As most women do, she used a measuring cup (some even use a funnel). I thought there must be an easier way of doing this.

"I decided to take an old, plastic, liquid soap container with the tip cut off, and see if this would work.

"It does!"

### Starch Right

"Since our company makes a number of popular brands of starch and likes to have satisfied customers, we have done considerable research on how starches are best used.

"First of all, women should realize there are two sets of variables—price and finish desired!

"In a somewhat ascending price and convenience scale there are the dry (to be cooked), the dry (to be mixed with hot water), the instant cold water starch, liquid starches, and new spray starches. Each has its virtues and devoted users.

"As to the finish desired—the cooked and hot water types of starches are best for stiff-collar-and-shirt results. They, of course, can be diluted for garments such as aprons.

"Instant cold water starch produces a more moderate,

crisp, pliable finish which is nice for most family washes. It can also be poured into the washer during the last rinse cycle right out of the box with no precooking or mixing. The washer assures that the starch is evenly distributed and therefore there are no spots from the starch. Liquid starches are more convenient for washing machine use, but are heavier to tote and cost more.

"Spray starches are even more convenient, but even we don't recommend using them for the whole wash from sheets to shirts, to dresses and aprons—too expensive for that! But they are wonderful and practical indeed for small things.

"Spray starch can be sprayed and then ironed for crisping of collars, cuffs, pressing out wrinkles in skirts, and so forth.

"A word about 'seasoning':

"Dry your articles; then sprinkle and leave in a dampened condition several hours before ironing. This is to assure even dampness. Starched items which are semidried (to the ready-to-iron-stage) in a dryer do not need to be held and seasoned since they are evenly moist.

"More starch is needed to obtain the same results when using a dryer.

"Finally, starch not only imparts a pleasing finish to fabrics, but it actually makes for easier soil removal. The starch keeps the dirt and grime on the surface—locks out dirt—so that it is washed off of, not out of material!"

### Press, Don't Iron

Ironing and starching are fine—when you have to. Now I want to talk to all of you tired women who iron pillowcases.

I agree with you—they should be ironed. I even like them lightly starched. But some days you just don't have the time. I found a new easy way to get the results of ironing—without the work.

I have box springs and mattresses like most of us do these days. So when I take my pillowcases out of the dryer—and I never let them *overdry*—I immediately fold them and carry them into the bedroom. I lift up a corner of the mattress and flop the folded pillowcases between the box spring and mattress!

I just let them stay there until the following week. I have found this to be the most energy-free pressing job you can find! Puts a lovely crease in them, too.

I am now using this method to press my sheets, too.

After all, we strip a bed and do the laundry each week. It's far easier than ironing, for us to lift up a corner of the mattress. We've got to anyway.

Just put a foot on the box spring and hold that mattress up with your knee. Put that folded sheet and those pillowcases which belong to that very bed under it. Then forget about them until the next changing time.

This is the greatest. Not only do you save time by not ironing them, but they are right there when you are ready to change that bed. Saves walking to the linen closet each week and according to how many beds you have, also saves lots of closet space.

### ✂ *Sew Be It*

"When my wife sews and stops for awhile—sometimes for days—she used to stick the needle under a few strands of thread on the spool.

"Sometimes the needle would split the thread or fall out. So I took one of my cigarettes, broke the filter off and stuck it into the hole in the spool.

"This makes a swell pincushion for the needle and it stays in place."

"Did you know that when you are sewing by hand, if you always sew towards yourself, it is much easier and your thread will not knot as badly?"

"When knitting, try using regular bobby pins as markers. These are always available and easy to take off your knitted piece without removing the needles or tearing the yarn.

"Hook the bobby pin through the stitch and let it dangle. It won't come off until you take it off."

### Gifts Galore

Doesn't it seem that the gals in the office are always getting married, celebrating anniversaries, changing jobs —*always* doing something that means a gift is in order? Well don't buy it; make it yourself!

How about place mats? "I love pretty pretty place mats and have found that corduroy and nylon net too, are the answer. They're machine washable and come in many lovely colors.

"I cut the material in various shapes and decorate the edges with my zig-zag attachment. Then I just trim the excess material close to the stitching. This gives a finish that won't ravel even after repeated laundering.

"These can't be purchased and they make such lovely gifts."

"By the way, when making things from corduroy, velvet, velveteen, or nappy wools, put your pattern on the smooth side of the material! It's much easier to get the pattern pinned on properly."

And for those bridal showers we're always getting invited to: "Here's a darling idea for bridal showers.

"Wrap individually bottles of vinegar, rubbing alcohol, and household bleach, a nylon net dish cloth, a Heloise pompon, a set of Heloise nylon net place mats—and a few other necessities. On the top of each package I print, 'Guess what this is?'

"There was not one thing that the bride would not need when her housekeeping started."

### Mend Your Ways
Remember, gals, at work, a safety pin won't take the place of stitches.

"My extension-course teacher taught me to remove the hem marks from man-made fabrics by rubbing them with white vinegar and then pressing.

"I always use a cloth over them when ironing, as man-made fabrics are usually delicate."

"When you turn down a skirt waistband to make the skirt shorter, turn the belt inside towards your body instead of turning it over on the outside. The result is much neater. No puckers or bulges show."

"So many skirts that have a back pleat cannot be shortened without making the pleat too short and ruining the looks of the skirt.

"My remedy is to rip the pleat out where it is stitched and just continue sewing the original back seam down to the bottom of the skirt. This eliminates the pleat completely. Cut the pleat away, leaving some allowance as in a skirt seam."

"When I had to shorten a plastic raincoat, I used three-quarter inch plastic tape on both sleeves and hem and it stayed indefinitely."

"I lined my skirt with an old half slip.

"I just took out the elastic and opened the left side seam for the zipper and sewed it to the waist band of my new skirt. It worked great, and I like it much better than regular lining."

### Top Sewing

If you dislike everyday-wear cotton blouses that are manufactured nowadays without pockets, do what I do. I buy blouses with long or roll-up sleeves, then cut off the bottoms of the sleeves and use the excess material to make pockets.

"My husband wears out the left pocket of his white shirts very fast. He takes his pen out of that pocket so many times a day the clip tears the top edge.

"I now remove the right pockets (they're always in good shape) from his old worn white shirts and replace that worn-out left pocket on an otherwise good shirt.

"Since I've started this, our shirt bill has been much less."

"I am a saleswoman. The other day I sold a lady six pairs of men's nylon replacement pockets. I remarked that she was going to do a lot of repair work.

"Much to my surprise she said they were for her own dresses and slacks that didn't have pockets!

"By opening the side seams, she sews in the pockets. Since these pockets are thin, they don't alter the appearance of the dress or slacks.

"I tried it on a pair of old slacks, and it really worked. So nice to have a pocket in which to keep cigarettes, lighter, or what have you."

"I am a seamstress and would like to pass on this tip:

"When altering, letting out, or taking in seams—sew the new seam before taking out the old.

"Your material will stay in place with no slipping."

"When making buttonholes (cotton material only), try running a line of colorless nail polish over the buttonhole area before cutting the material in the center of it, and no frayed edges will appear!"

"Use dental floss to sew snaps on garments.

"I think snaps are far better than a hook and eye on the back of a dress. They will not come loose and they don't get caught during dry cleaning either, or pulled loose like hooks and eyes do when they catch on other things.

"Moreover, it's far easier to snap a snap than it is to try to fasten a hook and eye!

"I happen to work for one of the biggest department stores in the nation, and this is our worst complaint.

"We have also found from the complaints in our department that snaps will never catch the back of a woman's hair.

"I feel that women could well utilize this idea on the garments that they make themselves. I do suggest, however, buying big snaps instead of small ones. They are much easier to snap by yourself and don't require that 'someone else' do you up."

This is a great idea. Some of us do have long hair. That hook and eye always gave me a problem.

### ❦ Get Hip

When it comes to housekeeping, please take my advice. Rome wasn't built in a day, and neither do you have to clean house that way. You working gals, especially, just can't.

Take your time when it comes to cleaning. Just do it when you are in the mood (and no one but you will know when that cleaning mood hits). Quit worrying about what other people think. You don't owe it to your neighbor, mother-in-law, or the boss' wife to keep a spotlessly clean house.

I have yet (and I am 48) to have any guest look under my beds to see if there was dust. So, don't knock yourself into a tizzy or have a nervous breakdown trying to keep it perfect. If you were perfect, you probably wouldn't be here. Think that over!

Some days I think that Scarlett O'Hara was much smarter than we are when she said, "I'll worry about it to-morrow . . . after all, tomorrow is another day."

I suggest that if you *have* to do spring cleaning, try cleaning only one room at a time. Don't allow yourself to do more than one room in any one week. Even if you're still in the mood, *quit* and just look back over what you have accomplished and enjoy it.

Here's why: We often use up too much energy at one time. This leads to overexertion and getting into a run-down condition (and, gals, I have heard many a doctor use that exact phrase when he diagnosed pneumonia and nerves).

When you start cleaning out closets, drawers, and cupboards, if you find you haven't used a certain article in a year, you probably won't use it for the next ten. Get rid of it. When it comes to really sorting out, there can be a method to your madness. Call your local charity organization; they can use those articles.

Each time you walk through a room and find something out of place, put it in your pocket. As you pass through the room where it belongs, deposit it in its proper place.

If you have a job during the week, weekends are the

best time to do heavy cleaning, where lots of hard labor is involved. Your family is there to help you, and if they join in the work and the fun, they appreciate the cleanliness so much more.

And it's a proven fact: If they help clean up, they will help keep it cleaner *thereafter*, which will prevent backaches for *you*.

All the electrical gadgets you buy and all the ammonia, kerosene, bleach, soap, and other cleansers in this entire world won't put that shine in your husband's eyes. Nor in the eyes of your children or your mother-in-law.

Budget your energy doing only what you can. Life is priceless, so learn to enjoy it. Learn to do things the easy way. Take every shortcut you can find.

As long as your family has good food to eat, some clean clothes to wear, and an *untired* mother who is jolly and understanding, there will be fewer doctor bills and fewer tranquilizers (which cost a heck of a lot of money and don't really *solve* our problems anyway).

Just be yourself, and do what you can. The world still goes on whether you mop under your bed or not. It's been that way for thousands of years, and will continue for ages to come.

# Chapter 2

# ❧ Working Mama

Whether you work full time or part, for charity or for profit, at home or away, I'll bet your heart is really with your family. And families take work—more work, sometimes, than you think you can fit into your busy schedule. Evening doesn't mean leisure time, as this all too typical letter points out:

"The wives in our neighborhood decided to tell you how we spend our 'leisurely' evenings. . . .

"Six o'clock: Work still not done. Washing machine has two loads to go. Hamburgers not thawed. Haven't reached the middle of the ironing basket, much less the bottom.

"Teen-agers' transistors are blaring three different programs. Books thrown on the coffee table, sweaters across the chairs, lunch box on the sofa.

"Husband comes home. Doesn't add anything to our day

24

because he's grouchy, wants to know where supper is, and why the paper is torn up. And why we didn't change the baby 'cause he's wet (we just did half an hour ago). He plops in a chair, takes off his shoes, throws them under the footstool, and demands that we keep the kids quiet.

"And while we're trying to get supper, the little ones come to mother—not daddy—with, 'Mother, how do you do this . . . ?' And what mother can give a sensible or logical answer while she's worried about the hamburger burning, and whether she will have time to fix daughter's dress for that school program?

"After supper, there are dishes to do, kids to be bathed, fights to settle. There's the garbage to take out, kitchen floor to mop, ashtrays to be emptied, school clothes to be ironed. How we long to settle down in the living room with the new magazine that came in the mail!

"No wonder we wives get disgusted. We feel that no one notices anything at all that we've accomplished, much less appreciates it. And that's why we hope fervently that if there is such a thing as reincarnation, that next time we'll be a man!"

It all sounds so familiar I can't help chuckling. I know the feeling; hoping you would be able to get everything done, yet knowing that some of it will never be finished. When these problems pile up, they seem larger-than-life and we feel so put-upon. Just keep on reminding yourself that you are not alone in these problems and that getting everything done is not nearly as important as keeping a sense of humor—and making your home a *happy* place.

And remember, there are ways to cut down the time of your labor without cutting down on the enjoyment your loved ones derive from it. With a little trickery and a lot of love, you part-time mamas can be full-time terrific.

*Working Mama*   25

## ☙ Safety First

Your first and probably most important job is to create a safe home. Well, *stop*, look and *read!*

So many times little children (especially the very young ones) cannot read, or do not heed, cautions on containers. Many times, too, mothers and fathers do not read directions and cautions on bottles and containers. Some bottles do not even have the words "poison," "caustic," or "toxic" written on them even though their contents can kill or cripple.

So here's what I figured out for you mothers and fathers who have little children. (It's also a good safety precaution for yourselves.)

Don't delay. Go buy some dark red fingernail polish at your dime store. Take the little brush out of that bottle of dark red fingernail polish and completely *paint* every

bottle cap and lid on such things as bleaches, ammonia, turpentine, kerosene, alcohol, disinfectants, insect sprays, spot removers, and cleaners. Include everything that would harm a child if swallowed. (The next time you buy a new bottle of bleach, ammonia, or disinfectant, all you have to do is remove that pretty red "caution" top from the empty one and screw it on the new bottle.)

*Also* paint a big "X" with that dark red fingernail polish on *both sides* of all these bottles and containers.

*Teach* your child *now* that anything he sees with a red mark—either an "X" or a red cap or lid on it—means *"NO-*

NO!"—"*Danger,* or *poison.*" Later, when he learns to talk and understand, you can explain it to him further.

He will use and reuse this red signal all his life. Even before he starts school, he will learn that a red light means "stop," or "danger." (Later, when he drives a car and sees the red stoplights of a car in front of him go on, he will know what it means.)

And let me give you another little hint for all young mothers who have small babies. Now is the time to take that bottle of fingernail polish and paint the *hot water faucet* in your bathtub, in your basin, and in your kitchen sink!

With your teaching, the little child will quickly learn that a *red* water faucet means *DANGER.* Don't forget, a little child sometimes does not know his left hand from his right, or a left faucet from a right one. At least the poor little tyke will know that *hot* water is coming out instead of that cold water he expects when he goes to wash his hands. This will prevent many scaldings.

Don't worry about putting fingernail polish on your metal water faucets. It won't hurt them one bit. As soon as the child is old enough to clearly remember which is hot water and dangerous, all you have to do is take some fingernail polish remover and remove the red polish with some facial tissue. It comes off the faucets clean as a whistle, no matter how long it's been on.

Let's save a life and prevent injury any way we can, because health cannot be bought for any amount of money.

### ❦ P.S. I Love You

"My husband works evenings and comes home from work very late. Since I have to get up early to get to my job and to get our children off to school, I don't always wait up for him.

"If there is something I want to tell him I leave a note. The only place I can be positive he'll look is on the bathroom mirror when he brushes his teeth.

"So I take a sheet of plastic wrap and put it on the mirror (it sticks by itself) and write the note on that with a felt marker. Then if he needs to write an answer, he just writes it on the bottom portion and I see it in the morning.

"The plastic wrap peels off the mirror easily."

### 🐟 Down the Hatch

"I've found that a muffin tin makes a wonderful tray in the refrigerator for baby bottles and opened jars of baby food.

"The bottles don't tip and spill, and by using a large tin, the day's supply of milk and the small jars of baby food are always within easy reach. The 'tray' can be slid in and out as needed, and the small jars are not always hidden behind larger containers."

"I use a stretch coaster (either bought or made from a sock top) on my new daughter's bottle to keep the milk warm until she finishes it."

"When I took my baby off baby food I used quick-cooking cereals for breakfast, but before I could cool the cereal, the baby would be hungry and crying.

"Now I've learned to drop an ice cube in the hot cereal, stir only a few seconds, then remove the remainder of the cube and the cereal is ready to eat.

"As most hot cereals cook rather thick, the melting cube doesn't make it too thin."

"I keep a roll of bathroom tissue by my baby's high chair for fast clean-ups while I am feeding him. It's more

economical than paper towels and not scratchy on his little face, either."

### Milk Woes

"A hint for mothers who have trouble getting their children to drink instant powdered milk: "I put one-half teaspoon of vanilla, two teaspoons of sugar, and a dash of nutmeg in a quart of instant milk.

"The children think it's eggnog and ask for more."

### 🐾 Taste Tempters

"My preschool youngsters are always wanting a drink of fruit juice or some kind of drink between meals.

"So when I do the breakfast dishes, I wash and scald some baby food jars and fill them with juices for the children to last the rest of the day. I stack these on the bottom shelf in my refrigerator within easy reach of my small ones.

"Sure saves, 'Mama, where is something to drink?' and my having to stop what I'm doing and pouring them something."

And look at the utility bills you will save on refrigeration! I have seen my children open the door and just stand there trying to figure out what they want. Then some-times spill it on the floor.

Too, those little jars can be set in tomato cartons and it makes for a much neater refrigerator. They slide in and out like a drawer, and don't tip over. Just be sure the lids are on the jars.

"Don't throw away those little plastic tubs that some margarines come in. They are great as cereal bowls, especially if you have a lot of little ones. If they are dropped they will not break. They are also very good for hot soups, and don't get soft like some plastic bowls."

### Mess Preventers

"As our TV is in the living room, I never allowed my active three-year-old to take anything to eat in there. That is, until I came up with the idea of letting him eat his snacks sitting *inside* one of the old corrugated boxes he dearly loves to play in.

"Now, if anything crumbles or spills, the box prevents accidents to our lovely carpet.

"After he's through, he stands up in the box while I brush him off. Then I just empty the crumbs into the wastebasket and the box is ready for playing with again."

"I found a way to give my children all the hot cocoa they want on school mornings without any messy pots to clean!

"In a large canister I make cocoa mix. I stir about three parts dry whole milk with one part powdered cocoa (the kind I buy has some powdered milk in it) and some sugar.

"Then I put my powdered mixture in the cup—I keep a coffee measure in the canister for this—then just fill it up with very hot tap water.

"Children don't want boiling hot cocoa anyway. This is easily made by my boys whenever they need a warm-up."

Fill a sterilized baby nipple with water from the baby's bottle and put it upside down in a small glass in your freezer. When put back on the little darling's bottle it makes the best teether ever.

If you have white sediment on your baby bottles from hard water, just boil them for 10 minutes or so in a big kettle of water to which a cup or two of vinegar has been added. Just how long you leave them in will depend on how much sediment you have on the glass.

To mark your baby bottles when going to visit a friend with a young baby in the house, try putting rubber bands around *your* baby's bottles.

After baby has outgrown his rubber teether, why not tie it to a pull toy?

When baby first starts to eat, try using a teacup instead of a bowl. It's much easier to hang onto (since you can put your finger through the handle) and saves many a broken dish.

New mothers who don't use an infant seat to bathe baby in are really missing an enjoyable, relaxed time. So is baby. Remove the pad and buckle strap and place a large folded bath towel in the seat. Place the little darling in the seat, pick both up, and place them in the water. Now you can use both hands, which is safer.

Roll up the sleeves of nighties and sweaters when putting them on those little waving arms, and it will be much easier for you and baby too.

For tired working mothers, who are sick of trying to save on baby and junior foods:

After each meal, if you have any leftover vegetables, stewed fruits, or scrambled eggs, put each dab in a baby food jar and set in the refrigerator. Next day when meal-time comes around, just set the jars in your baby bottle sterilizer! They fit perfectly.

If you leave the tops off, they will warm up in a jiffy and even moisturize the food. (It's the steam, you know.) Sure will save on your budget.

### ❦ The Hot Seat

Here's a great way to solve your seating space problems and make the kiddies happy too:

"When I have company for dinner and don't have enough table space for all the children, I get out my adjustable ironing board and put it low enough for the smaller ones to use. I just place a cloth over it and make it 'their' table.

"This handy adjustable ironing board eliminates the need for stacking books on a chair so the little tyke can reach his dinner. No matter whether the children sit on pillows, stools, or the floor, the board may be adjusted to any height to fit their needs."

### ❦ Take 'em to the Movies

When eating at a drive-in—especially if you have a batch of children—don't order all hamburgers or all tuna-fish sandwiches. Mix them up a little!

Last weekend I ordered tuna fish, my daughter got roast beef. We asked that they either cut them in half or bring us a knife to cut them with.

Then we each had part of two different sandwiches. This is a surefire solution for fussy eaters.

Now, as another little afterthought, if you wrap your oldest paring knife in a paper napkin and keep it in your glove compartment, you can cut your own sandwiches anytime, either in halves or in fourths. And just think, if you have a big family, it will really be like eating from a party plate.

Why not bring some popcorn, too?

"I make my own popcorn for the movies. I save dry cereal boxes (and milk cartons) and fill them with freshly-popped corn. The wax liner in the box prevents the butter from coming through."

### *Thirsty Little Travelers*

"When we are out driving with our small children, they invariably want to stop every few miles for a drink of water. This is quite upsetting to Dad.

"I saved some of those little plastic lemon and lime juice squeeze bottles that are flat on one side. First, I removed the insert with my ice pick. Then I rinsed them out and filled them with water. After putting the screw cap back on, I marked each child's name on his own little bottle.

"The children absolutely love them. They can drink out of the tiny spout without spilling anything. If they want only a sip, the top may be screwed back on. And they fit so easily in the glove compartment."

### *Moms- and Pops-to-be*

"I heard the other day about a mother-to-be who, when preparing her things for the hospital, also prepared a box for her husband!

"It contained *his* favorite magazines, goodies for munching, and change for the telephone."

"We just had our first baby and while my wife was given many showers, the greatest gift of all was a little card which said, 'This entitles you to two weeks of free diaper service!' "

"I save empty powder boxes for the nursery. I think it is much easier to puff powder on the baby instead of sprinkling it on.
"The puff stops powder buildup in the creases of skin because you can apply it more evenly.
"Naturally, I fill the box with baby powder and use a brand-new puff.

"If you want to dry baby's plastic pants in a hurry, place them in the hood of your hair dryer! They dry in a few minutes and are soft and warm to put back on the baby."

"I have found the empty roll-on deodorant bottles make very good containers for baby oil or baby lotion. You can just roll a small amount on baby and smooth it with the fingers.
"So much easier than pouring it from the bottle, and there's no waste at all."

### Happy Sleep
Guess you working gals, especially, hope the little one sleeps comfortably through the night. It's certainly no fun running out in the morning after being up every other hour with baby. These tricks are bound to help some:
"When our baby was tiny and couldn't find his pacifier once it got away from him, I was up half a dozen times at night helping him in his search.
"Then I got smart. Using heavy carpet thread, I whipped the ring portion of his pacifier to the tip of the head of his stuffed, terry cloth clown doll.

"In no time at all our boy was finding his pacifier by himself even in his groggiest moments. I've seen him locate the doll, turn it to the proper position to get the pacifier and not open an eye!

"It also gave him something to cuddle and could be washed by just pulling the pacifier apart."

"To keep my baby warm on cold nights, I remove the mattress from the baby bed and spread a large blanket or quilt over the springs as a liner. Then I bring it up and over the sides of the crib, pinning it very securely on the outside at each corner around the top rung.

"Next I put the mattress back in the crib.

"This keeps drafts out and cold air from coming up from the floor around the mattress. A warm baby sleeps better!"

"Our baby was a winter nursing baby.

"I kept the heating pad beside his crib and when I took him up for a night feeding, I turned the pad on warm and laid it in his bed.

"When I put him back in his little crib I removed the heating pad. Because the bed was so nice and warm he settled down more quickly than he used to in a cold bed."

"Here's what I did with one of my old formals:

"I made a fancy dust ruffle for our baby's crib. The full skirt of the dress made the actual ruffle. An inexpensive piece of cotton, which I purchased in the same shade, is perfect under the mattress where it doesn't show.

"The dust ruffle is both decorative and useful since it provides hidden, extra storage space beneath the crib."

### Wash-up Time

Babies can seem as slippery as eels, particularly to new mothers:

"I found an easy, no-slip way to bathe a small baby. I bought one of those inexpensive, plastic baby bathtubs and then slipped a regular pillowcase over the *whole* tub!

"It forms a perfect soft hammock to lay my baby in for a sponge bath or a regular bath. And all the used water drains through the pillowcase into the tub.

"It leaves me with both hands free. The baby is secure and it keeps the water from splashing."


Whatever it is that small children have against washing, these hints should go a long way in breaking down their resistance:

"Small boys seem to have such an aversion to washing their faces! At least our little cowboy did until we came up with the idea of giving him one of Daddy's old shaving brushes! He works up a good lather, then smears it all over his wet face—some of it even gets in his ears and on his neck!

"The brush gets the lather into the pores for good cleaning, and it feels so good that he takes quite a while to give himself his 'shave' facial.

"Naturally, he washes the lather off when he's finished playing with the shaving brush. To be most effective, the child should be able to watch the process in a mirror."


"Like all small children, my little ones have trouble putting the towel back on the bar in the bathroom.

"I bought another towel bar and had my husband attach it to the wall two feet from the floor, *under* the regular one. So there would be no overlap, he moved the regular bar up about a foot.

"We use the higher bar and the children enjoy their own mini-towel rack."

### Baby Shoes Too

"When you purchase new white baby shoes, before your 'bundle of joy' wears them, take a bottle of clear nail polish and cover the brown edge of the sole all the way around.

"Then when the shoes need to be polished, you don't have to worry about getting white on the soles because all you have to do is wipe it off with a damp cloth.

"You'll always have neat-looking shoes, and you never need to polish the dark rim of the sole!"

Here's another money saver:

"When baby starts outgrowing those nice terry-cloth stretch outfits with the feet, here's a way of prolonging their life a bit.

"I cut only the heels and toes out, leaving enough in the middle to have a strap (like stretch pants). Then I let him wear them with shoes and socks. Great on the budget!"

### Dressing Quickies

Picture a morning you're late for work, you're helping the children dress, and you can't tell Janie's clothes from Johnny's:

"I use X marks to distinguish between the children's clothing. The oldest child is X, second child is XX, etc.

"When the clothes are handed down, I simply add another X to designate the new owner."

Cut down your ponytail-making time:

"While brushing my little daughter's hair, a rubber band broke, and I asked my son to bring me another. He brought several and said, 'Put these extra ones on the brush handle, so next time you'll have *some handy!*'"

Best of all, a way to make struggling with those overshoes no struggle at all:

"I am a kindergarten teacher and I've huffed and puffed when struggling to put rubbers and overshoes on my wriggling, spaghetti-legged youngsters. No more!

"I now put the shoes inside of the rain boots *first*, then have the children step in the shoes. Sure is easier."

### Do-it-themselves

The best time-saver of all is *teaching* your little ones to do things for themselves!

"Children are often able to put on their own shoes, and even tie them, before they are able to distinguish the right shoe from the left.

"Simply make a small mark on the inside curved edge of each shoe sole with a felt-tipped pen, putting it so that it doesn't touch the ground as the child walks. Then, match the marks side-by-side—and presto, shoes are lined up perfectly.

"A small child can quickly learn to match the marks."

### Tips for Play

Know those darling little kiddie pools that are so inexpensive? When they spring a leak—or the hard plastic cracks—*don't* discard them. They make the most wonderful sandboxes imaginable! They are easy to move around because they're small.

Another good thing about them is that when it gets too bad to play outside, the sandbox can be moved into the garage or put on the porch. And in winter, it can be brought down into the basement so the children can play the year round. (Sacks of sand can be bought at lumber yards and garden shops.)

Put those covers from spray cans to use:
"Save them until summer for the children to use in their

sandpile or play pool. My grandchildren had a wonderful time with them last year making mudpies and building castles."

"If you like to put baby's playpen out in the yard but have no shade tree to put it under, try stretching a big sheet across your clotheslines and pinning it at four corners.

"Then just place the playpen under the sheet. It keeps the hot sun from shining directly on baby."

"I cut squares of gauze in different sizes, wet them, then put them in separate plastic bags and freeze them. They're ready to apply to bumps or bruises when needed.

"The children appreciate them because they are not hard and lumpy as ice cubes in a bag."

## 🦷 School Days

"For those who send money to school with a small child, tape the coin to the inside of the lid of his lunch box.

"This way the money is never lost."

"When teaching your young children to print their name, remember that first graders don't print in all capital letters. They begin to learn the difference in upper and lower case letters from the first day.

"So teach your child to print 'Sharon' rather than 'SHARON,' for it shakes up a youngster when the teacher tells him he can't print the way he was taught at home!"

## 🦷 Happy Birthday to All

Nothing delights a child more than a birthday party, especially his own. Make your kiddy party the talk of the neighborhood: .

"Instead of putting candles on a birthday cake, I count the number of children who will be there and put that

many colored toothpicks on the cake. Then I tape a number on each one making them look like little flags.

"After the cake and ice cream, the children are given a prize to match the number on their toothpick. It certainly beats having wax blown all over the place!"

For little kiddies with dirty fingernails: Before using a nail file to scrape the dirt out, scrape their nails along a bar of soft bar soap, then wash their hands. The dirt is loosened and the result is cleaner nails.

When cutting the fingernails of a small child who wiggles, wait until after he is asleep, it's much easier and a lot safer. They usually are such sound sleepers, they never know what's going on.

For children who wear glasses part of the time and are always misplacing them, use a name and address label. Stick it on the inside of the earpiece and cover it with cellophane tape. If lost, they will be immediately returned. This is especially good on dark glasses.

When washing a child's hair, always give him a *dry* washcloth to hold over his forehead. This will absorb the soapy water and prevent it from running into his eyes as he leans over the basin.

When my baby was small, his vitamin drops often ran out of his mouth before he figured out how to swallow them.

I discovered that if I put his pacifier in his mouth immediately after he took his drops, he would suck and naturally swallow all his vitamins.

Have you ever tried putting instant potatoes in soup for babies? It gives more "body" to soup and is nourishing, too. Our daughter is starting to feed herself and she likes it this way.

### ❦ Tidbits for Mommy

Here are some tidbits from other mothers which I only wish I had known when my children were little:

"Instead of throwing your diapers in a basket when you take them off the line, put them over your arm or shoulder. Much easier to fold and far less wrinkles."

"Never hang just one diaper on the clothesline by itself. Hang two at a time, one over the other. Saves clothesline space and half your time. Great when folding two together for that last change of the day."

"Fill any bottle with a finger-type plunger with water. Always keep this by the baby's bed. Keep another in your baby's diaper bag. Wonderful for changing soiled diapers. Just spray away, either on a cloth, paper tissue, or directly on the 'object' itself. Saves running to the faucet for water for that cleaning job. . . ."

"If the diaper pins are hard to push through my baby's diapers, I just run the end of the pin through my hair (my head is always there) and then pin away. It goes through the diaper as slick as a whistle."

And another mother wrote:
"A bar of soap with the wrapper left *on* is wonderful for sticking diaper pins in. They push through that diaper like lightning. When the bar of soap gets all chipped and broken, it can always be used for something else. By leaving the wrapper on the soap, chips don't spill over everything."

And a granddaddy told us:
"Don't ever leave loose diaper pins laying around where your namesake can get hold of them. They are dangerous. Take a key chain and attach it to the bassinet or somewhere close by and fasten the pins through this. Just be sure those pins are out of baby's reach. Too, you can always find a diaper pin if the old one breaks. And they do."

From a new teen-age mother:
"Oh, Heloise, how wrong I was to think that a college diploma would diaper my two babies and stretch my budget! Now I am using my old plastic purse for a diaper bag and find it far better than the expensive diaper bag I got at our first baby shower. The handle is stronger, and it's all lined in plastic, and it's free."

And another Mama says . . .
"As the mother of seven, I hit upon this hint today purely because of my baby crying for his supper. When heating strained baby food, I've found that it sometimes gets watery and is very difficult to feed to the baby.

"Tonight I had a box of baby cereal on the table and sprinkled a couple of teaspoons in the strained baby food. This thickened it immediately and made feeding a snap.

"From my baby's point of view, it certainly did not affect the taste, as he finished the jar with no balking.

And the last, but not the least, is one from a teen-age father which I think is priceless:

"We have two babies. My sweetheart uses a shoe tote bag to carry the offsprings' diapers and baby bottles when we go out. It not only looks neat but holds lots of stuff. It can be thrown over the shoulder, and it's much smaller than an ordinary diaper bag too."

And may I give my special blessing to all mothers, whether new or old. Those little angels which you are rearing will run the world in the next generation.

# Chapter 3

# ❦ My Fair Lady

It's unfair that working gals, who have to be seen in public so much, are the ones with the least time for beauty and grooming. Though we all want to look nice for our families, they'll always love us, even if our nail polish *is* chipping a bit.

But appearance on the job really counts! If you work in an office, naturally, your boss is going to want a well-groomed, attractive you to welcome his clients.

Even for volunteer work, what you look like *matters*. Who's more likely to get that committee chairmanship, the sloppily dressed woman with stringy hair or the one who can be introduced proudly at the big luncheon?

There's no getting away from it, you're going to have to look your most beautiful self. And you're going to have to find some neat tricks to fit easily into your busy day.

### ♥ *Hair Glow*

Let's start at the top, gals. Are you aware when using a concentrated shampoo (either in tube or bottle form) which says, "Wet hair completely, then apply shampoo," that if you put a glop of thick shampoo on your palms and rub them together, then rub on your wet hair, that it distributes the shampoo more evenly?

Many wonderful beauty operators write that most concentrated shampoos can also be diluted with warm water before using. They suggest that women with a heavy head of hair use this method. Many beauticians also recommend rinsing long, thick hair in good old vinegar! Use one-fourth cup of vinegar to three-fourths cup of water. Then a slight water rinse.

From one working gal to another, a professional beautician sent me some clues for the shampoo to beat all shampoos:

"I am the owner of a beauty salon. Many women can only afford us once a month or so. Therefore, I would like to give them a few tips about shampooing their hair.

"The hair should be brushed vigorously before any shampoo is even attempted.

"Also, it ought to be sudsed at least twice—three times

for excessively oily hair—and thoroughly rinsed after each sudsing.

"After the shampoo is worked into a lather of suds, take the hairbrush and use it vigorously along the hairline from the front of the head, along the sides, and clear across the back neckline—that's where it's most oily. You will get a far better shampoo."

If you find that your neck gets greasy and oily before the rest of the hair does, the reason, according to a state board cosmetologist, is that this is where the nerve centers and oil glands are.

To remove this oiliness and greasiness between shampoos, I pour plain old rubbing alcohol on a dry washcloth and just rub away. I do this only along the back of the neck where the hair is oily.

While the hair along the neckline is still damp from the rubbing alcohol, I roll it up in pin curls immediately. I find that the alcohol will dry much faster than water because it evaporates more quickly.

For those who wear heavy make-up and get oil around their hairline, rubbing alcohol can be used there, too. Unless you're allergic to rubbing alcohol (and I have never known anyone who is) this is a wonderful method.

Remember now: Do *not* try to give yourself a whole shampoo with rubbing alcohol. Just dampen the washcloth and rub the oily hair between the folds of the washcloth.

### Ready, Set, Go!

A working gal has a quick-set idea great for helping you keep an important business appointment when you haven't had time for a real set:

"When I want to set my hair in a hurry without getting

it thoroughly wet, I dampen my hair using a plunger-type spray bottle of water set aside for this very purpose.

"First I brush my hair thoroughly and comb it, then spray away with this fine mist of water. Then I roll it up and it dries ever so quickly."

Some of you gals seem to know just everything there *is* to know about hair care.

"When using a few curlers to pep up a hairdo, or between shampoos of the whole head, instead of wetting the hair, simply wet each roller. Give it two or three shakes to remove the excess water, then roll as usual.

"The dry hair will immediately stick to the roller and will roll perfectly and dry sooner for a nice touch-up hair-do."

If you have trouble sleeping when wearing curlers, here's a suggestion:

"Put the third or top half of your hair up on your curlers, then pin curl the rest of it."

"If you use different sizes of brush rollers for setting your hair, don't throw them away when the brushes wear down. Just remove the brushes from them and insert in the next smaller size."

Also, it's much handier if you get out your "plumber's helper," put it on the floor and stick the wig block on it. The hole in the bottom of the block exactly fits on the wooden handle of the "plumber's helper."

If you put both feet on the rubber part of the "helper," then resetting your wig is as easy as falling off a log, because you can use both hands and easily turn the wig around as needed.

### Hair Saver

A great hint about those new upright hair dryers for home use:

"In order to use mine, I had to sit in an uncomfortable straight chair to be at the proper height. The other day,

however, I discovered that I could sit in the most comfortable chair in the house and use the dryer by perching it on top of my adjustable ironing board!

"It sure makes drying time more pleasant. No hour wasted sitting in an uncomfortable position. I can relax nicely." I consider this idea a life-saver.

Ladies, be sure to take good care of your precious piece of equipment. If you have a hair dryer with a plastic hood, why don't you go get the hood right now and look at it? You will probably find that the inside of it is dirty.

Next time you wash your bath towels, turn the hood wrong side out and throw it in with the towels. The nap from the terry cloth towels will buff against it so that it will turn out beautiful and clean again.

I did not put mine in the dryer. I only washed it, put it back on the hair dryer, turned it on, and it dries all by itself.

Let's keep 'em clean, gals, they last longer.

"I've found a quick and easy way to dry nylon combs, brushes, and any other small item I forget to wash ahead of time. Just put them in the hood of a portable hair dryer and they'll dry in no time."

## Perm-a-curl

If you wash your hair a day or two before, you will have some of your own natural oil in it when you give yourself that permanent. I have used this method the last two times and it works perfectly.

Also, when shampooing your tresses, take your hair down before it is overdry, comb it, and then get it under the hair dryer again if you wish. This way even if any curl was rolled wrong, it will fall into place beautifully.

"When giving yourself a home permanent, if you have no one to call on to roll the neckline curls, try this:

"Cut the top from a nylon stocking, stretch it over your head until it is down to the neck. Then push it up to the level at the back where those pesky neckline curlers start. Slide the rat-tail end of the comb straight across your head and draw down only the hair needed. Then roll away.

"The nylon stocking holds the other hair up out of your way."

"When giving myself a home permanent the end papers used to create problems until I discovered this:

"Since my hands were already wet and sticky (that's the problem) I took the batch of end papers, folded them in the middle, thus making a crease. (The papers will be V-shaped.) Then I laid them over the inner edge of the sink.

"All I had to do then was just touch the papers with the thumb and index finger to pick one up. This saves time trying to fold the paper with your slick fingers."

"After putting your hair up for a home permanent, use

*My Fair Lady* 49

a stretch hair band around your head in front of the rollers and tuck it behind your ears.

"You'll be amazed that the solution does not run down your face, as these stretch bands are very absorbent.

"Also, you can tuck cotton or tissues between stretch band and hairline to further cut down drips."

### Easy-dye

A busy secretary suggests that "during the half hour or so waiting period when coloring hair, if you put some plastic wrap around the temples of your eyeglasses you won't stain them."

And I have an idea for those of you who dye your own eyelashes and brows. After years of doing this myself, I finally learned a good way to keep from getting the dye in my eyes. I now put my magnifying mirror down flat on the table and bend over while putting the dye on.

This way, if any of the dye spatters, it will not get back into the eyes as it does when looking into a dressing table or bathroom mirror.

### ✌ Bathing Beauty

"When I take a shower I use two shower caps, one larger than the other. The smaller one goes on first and the larger one goes *over* that.

"When the shower is over, I remove the top, drippy cap. The inner cap, which is perfectly dry, keeps my long hair from falling down and getting wet or in the way while I am drying myself."

"Two bottle caps from a soft drink bottle, pressed into a cake of soap will keep the soap dish from getting gooey and cuts down on soap waste. (Of course the family must be reminded to always put the soap cap-side down.)"

## Bath-science

When you use that glorious stuff for bubble baths, take a tip from me: Don't turn your water faucet in the bathtub on low or at the regular speed. Turn it on high! Let the bathtub get about an inch of water in it, *then* pour in that bubble bath. Watch the bubbles pile twice as high!

You will get more bubbles for your money, regardless of what you use as bubble bath.

Another money-saver: "This hint is for gals who love to use bath oil in their bath water—but find it too expensive.

"I use plain old baby oil. I just pour two capfuls into the tub while filling it."

A cute trick for using dusting powder: "When using bath powder, I stand in my bathtub to dust it on. No dusting powder flies anywhere except in the tub."

## 🐾 The Choppers

Here's something you gals should be sure to carry to work:

"A neat way to use mouthwash is to sterilize any plastic squeeze bottle you may have, then pour the mouthwash into it. When needed, just a squeeze or two will squirt the right amount into your mouth."

## 🐾 Glamour Puss

Whether you're behind a typewriter or a sales counter, before a class, or for that matter, your own kids, put your prettiest face forward.

As a working gal, you *can't* spend hours in front of the mirror. So heed my wise letter-writers:

"For a refreshing facial, buy a half pound of rolled, sterile cotton and cut it into four-inch squares. Pack these in a widemouthed jar. Then pour your favorite skin lotion over the cotton, and keep packing more cotton and adding more lotion until the jar is full.

"Cap the jar and keep in the refrigerator, and you are ready for a cool minute-facial any time. Sure makes your skin lotion last longer."

"From my boudoir comes a great suggestion for those who use face powder and buy it in boxes with a cellophane top:

"If you will take a soft drink can opener and open only one V-hole in that cellophane, as if you were opening a can, your powder puff will never be loaded with too much powder, and you can keep it inside the box."

You can also take a razor blade and cut an "X" in the center of the cellophane. As your powder supply goes down, you can make the slit bigger, giving you a perfectly powdered puff each time.

For ladies who prefer loose face powder:

"If you like to put your powder in a pretty box or glass jar, a piece of nylon net placed on top of the powder makes the perfect sifter so the loose powder won't fly away. It's also a wonderful filter that prevents you from getting too much powder on your puff."

### The Long Red Line
If you can't manage a lip brush and have trouble getting a clean line when you apply lipstick, just try rubbing it across an old emery board. Wow! Does it make a fine edge when you put on your lipstick! (It ruins the emery board, so use an old one that can be discarded.)

## ❦ Polish, Polish Everywhere

I'm no perfectionist when it comes to keeping my fingernails polished, I'm lucky if I get new polish on once a month.

For other busy working gals who have this same problem, here's what I finally learned to do. I put my emery board, fingernail polish remover, and polish next to my telephone. (Some of you *might* be able to get away with this at the office!) Now when the phone rings and I know I'm going to talk a bit, I pick up the emery board! If I only get one hand filed, that's at least some improvement. If the conversation goes on, I can file the other hand and perhaps get one coat of polish on. If it goes on and on and on, I can get that second coat on.

And last but not least, if I finally get the top coat on and it's dried a bit, I say, "There's somebody at the door, I just have to go."

So, to you gals who never seem to have time to keep your nails looking nice, this is one way to get it done.

(Another way I found was to keep all of this paraphernalia on my breakfast table. When my neighbor comes over for coffee, I take advantage of that time, too. It's also a good way to make use of your coffee breaks.)

"If you color your nails and want the polish to set in a few minutes, take a bowl of water and put it in the freezer until it is icy cold.

"Then after you put the polish on, dunk your nails into the icy water for about a minute or so. A quick and easy way to finish if you are in a hurry."

## Take It All Off

I was at a friend's house recently and saw her take a bottle of inexpensive nail polish remover and pour it into a small, empty cold cream jar. (I was completely flabbergasted.) Then she stuffed it half-full of little cotton balls, screwed the lid on tight and shook it. When she opened

it and picked out a cotton ball, she squeezed it a bit so the excess polish remover would drip back onto the other cotton balls in the jar. She used one to remove her fingernail polish. Whenever she gets near the bottom of the jar, she just adds some more cotton.

### ✌ *Eyebrows*

So many women wear bifocals and just cannot see to pluck their own eyebrows. A good way is to put a magnifying glass over your own hand mirror and just pluck away.

Another way is to either use a magnifying mirror or just turn your bifocals upside down! That sounds crazy, I know, but who cares as long as we can see?

If you are ever giving yourself a home permanent and can't get that slick off your hands, wash with soap and water, rinse, then apply vinegar. Presto, no slick. (This also works when using household bleach or any other slick product.)

When you wash your hair in the kitchen sink and have

lots of suds that won't go down the drain properly—have
you ever thought of turning on the disposal? Just watch
those suds disappear! (If you've got long hair, for heaven's
sake, don't leave that in.)

# Chapter 4

# ✿ Day Off?

A day off from the job usually means a day on at home! And that means getting to those projects—closet cleaning, furniture painting and refinishing, gardening, and what have you.

Now I know it isn't fun, sitting there drinking that cup of coffee and thinking, "My goodness, we've just got so much to do today." And so you have. But why don't you get a big smile on your face, let those cute wrinkles come up around your eyes, and think, "Now I am enthused, and so help me, Hannah, I'm going to clean at least one closet today."

The way to do it is to open that one closet door, take everything out and throw it on the bed. Do it before you think about it for too long. Once it's on the bed, you've got to finish. As you pick up each garment, ask yourself—

does this need a button? Has it been cleaned? Laundered . . . ?

Take anything that needs repairing, especially hand-sewing and drop it beside your favorite chair. Leave it there. Then while you're watching television some night, get *that* mending done! It takes little effort to do it when you're at ease sitting in your favorite chair. Effort is when you use your whole "day off" to do the mending. Why not do it while your husband is there watching you? He'll think you're a better housewife.

Now for the other stuff: Don't ever put *dirty* clothes back in your closet. Remember that perspiration, body oils, and soil will deteriorate most clothing. So, anything that has been worn once or twice, put on the rod in the middle of your closet.

This way, when you really need something to wear, but don't want to wear anything real special, you will know the clothes in the middle can be worn one more time before being cleaned or laundered.

And here's something else you're going to find along that rod in your closet—umpteen extra coat hangers! If

you get rid of those alone, you will have a great deal more closet space.

Clothes should not be crowded in a closet. You can bring something right back from the cleaners, hang it up in a jammed closet and it will get wrinkles.

Clutter is confusion. So let's get up and clean one closet.

Don't try to do two closets in one day. This will tire you out and make it a chore. And chores are what we don't like and can live without. You'll be so proud after having one closet thoroughly cleaned, that you'll want to keep it that way.

### ✎ Redo It for Today

Time out today for furniture remodeling:

"When you no longer have any use for an old-fashioned vanity that has drawers on either side, simply saw the drawers away from the mirrored center section.

"Presto! Two very nice nightstands."

This is exactly how the nightstands in my daughter's bedroom were made: After sawing out the mirror section, we also sawed off the legs, leaving only the ornamental part at the base of the dresser. It makes the stands look more modern. Then we sanded and refinished the sawed-off edges. The pulls on the drawers were pretty badly "beat-up," so we bought new ones at the dime store.

If you don't happen to have one of these old-fashioned dressers, scout around the secondhand stores. I'll bet you can pick one up for a song—we did!

Everyone who sees the nightstands is amazed that we did it ourselves.

Another neat trick for getting new furniture from old:

"The newer style homes are combining the living room and dining areas, and the type of furniture used in homes built about forty years ago is going out of style.

"My idea was to remove the legs from the buffet and china closet, and combine the two pieces.

"I placed the china closet on top of the legless buffet.

"All the wonderful space in the two pieces is valuable

storage space, and it's a beautiful piece of furniture which can be used either in the living room or in the dining area."

## ❦  Beautiful Windows

Many of us have a kitchen or bathroom window that doesn't have a good view. For instance, kitchen windows sometime look out on trash cans or alleys. Or perhaps you have other windows that you like to have light come through, but don't want people seeing in.

Why not frost them?

This will cost you only a few cents per window. Furthermore, it even saves washing windows each month, because the rain marks and the dust on the outside don't show!

Buy some Epsom salts. Get the smallest jar you possibly can because it goes a long way when dabbing windows with it. This should cost about twenty-five cents.

Pour about two heaping tablespoons in a saucer and add one tablespoon of beer to it. This will then foam. Let it set for at least thirty minutes. The salt crystals will partially dissolve. You will then end up with a liquid that looks like absolutely nothing, but it will make you an artist. And what an artist you're going to be!

Dip a piece of facial tissue into this liquid and wipe each window pane as if you were washing it.

Then while it is still thoroughly wet, go back and dab, dab and pat the pane with the wet tissue. It's going to look real messy. But you will get an artistic pattern which is exactly what you want. The most beautiful crystals will form on your window when it dries.

God's sunshine still comes through, but you can't see in from the outside and yet you can see out. Even the sun's glare is reduced. When you want to remove the crystals all you have to do is wash the window. Just plain water removes it.

There's one thing I must caution you about: your windowpanes must be clean. I recommend washing them with some ammonia water to remove all the carbon, then wiping dry with facial tissues. Don't use a bath towel, a dishcloth, or a sponge because these contain a minute amount of grease or body oil.

Give it a try. You'll not only have fun doing it, but you'll love the beautiful designs and enjoy the privacy, too!

When it comes to draperies, let's listen to the pros:

"I am an interior decorator and when I take draperies down for cleaning, I mark on the inside heading of each drapery: (window #1 right, #1 left,) etc. with an indelible ballpoint pen.

"As I take the drapery pins out, I use the ballpoint pen to put a dot where each pin will be reinserted. The ballpoint pen mark does not come out in the cleaning.

"When rehanging the draperies, I start in the center of the traverse rod, hooking onto the master carrier first.

"If extra carriers are on the rod, leave them at the outside ends of the rod or the draperies will not slide easily.

"These rules will save you a lot of hard work."

Here's another valuable tip: "We live in an apartment with very drafty windows.

"I use thin plastic garment bags to stuff in between the cracks around the windows to keep out the drafts. By cutting the plastic to fit, it doesn't show and it really stops the wind."

### ✎ Line It Lovely

You gals have more imaginative ways to line drawers than I ever thought possible:

"Did you know that corrugated cardboard is nice for lining the shelves of those metal cabinets most offices and homes have?

"I just cut pieces of the cardboard to fit, cover the tops of them with freezer paper (shiny side up), tape the paper under the edges of the cardboard, and presto!

"It's easy to clean, protects surfaces, and deadens noise."

This idea is absolutely fantastic! I had metal kitchen cabinets and was always bothered by the noise of pots, pans, and dishes banging around.

Not having freezer paper, I resorted to aluminum foil to cover the pieces of corrugated boxes.

Since my shelves are large, I cut the pieces of cardboard into sections and fit two or three sections on the large shelves. This way they can be removed for easy cleaning —wiping with that damp sponge or recovering with foil. No trouble at all.

This also keeps one from moving everything from the shelf to the drainboard while cleaning the entire cabinet!

"Kitchen paper toweling—which now comes quilted and in pretty pastel shades—makes excellent inexpensive lining for kitchen drawers and cupboard shelves.

"I use at least a double thickness of toweling. It is soft and sticks to the shelves without much fastening down. The toweling is easily folded into the proper shape which eliminates any cutting and fitting that one sometimes finds necessary for stiffer papers.

"It's also very economical."

A use for an old, discolored plastic tablecloth: "Wash the cloth, then use pinking shears to cut it to the proper size and shape for lining shelves. These are attractive and so easy to make and keep clean."

I've run across one of the most terrific ideas I think I have had in many a moon. I just finished laying carpets, and by the time you cut all of the "corners" there are bound to be a bunch of scraps left over. And I mean scraps, not big pieces that you can use for throw rugs. I cut these up and used them to line drawers!

Not only does this cut down on the noise (especially where you have those metal drawers) but gives a nice cushion to anything you might have in a drawer (such as a silverware divider tray) and keeps the stuff from sliding around. I also use some in the bottom of cabinets and on shelves.

I had one tiny piece left, and I used it to put on my kitchen windowsill. I don't know why, but everybody in every family always puts something on a windowsill, and the paint gets absolutely ruined.

So, let's don't ever throw away even a scrap of carpeting, no matter how small.

If you have those older-type homes where the cold air scoots under the window in winter and cool air from the air conditioning escapes in the summer, just try putting a little strip of the carpet right side up in the sill and then close that window. It makes the window fit snug as a bug in a rug.

Don't forget to air your pillows once in a while in the shade. Hot sun dries out the feathers.

If you put them in a dryer without heat and tumble them occasionally, they will come out ever so fluffy and and have a clean smell. In fact you might think you have new pillows.

If you have unexpected company and not enough beds for sleeping . . . you can always divide your mattress and box springs and get double sleeping space. Much more comfortable than pallets or folding cots. Put the mattress on the floor and leave the box springs on the bed.

Put a few extra blankets on the box springs for extra comfort so it will be softer.

Use your hair dryer hose to dust houseplants and plastic flowers. But be sure and do it before you do your dusting!

And anytime you defrost your chest-type freezer (or even one in the top of a refrigerator), try using that plastic dustpan to scoop all the "gloop" out with. It holds both the water and the chunks of ice.

The bathtub or shower stall are both good places to dump all this ice for melting, since your sink will probably be full of frozen foods.

I always line the bottom of my freezer compartment with two layers of waxed paper to keep the ice trays from sticking.

If your sofa or chair keeps sliding against the wall, try putting a thin piece of sponge under each leg. No more shuffling off to Buffalo! This also works under baby cribs and playpens. Especially when the child gets to that rock and roll stage!

Use a piece of leftover vinyl tile from your kitchen floor as a cutting board. It's easy on your good knives and can be washed in a jiffy and it's exactly the right size, too.

When storing those silky down comforters that refuse to stay folded, just put them in an old pillowcase. Keeps 'em clean, too. Some people roll them and then tie with an old nylon stocking.

If you paint your bathroom, place a thin plastic bag (dry-cleaner's type) over those mirrors, washbasin, bathtub, and toilet before ever starting that nasty job. Sure saves spatters galore.

Plastic wrap pieces can also be put on a portion of that bathroom mirror and just left there indefinitely (it adheres). When you take a bath or shower, that portion of the mirror won't steam up.

When painting baseboards, if you will use a dustpan with a rubber tip along the edge to push down the side of your wall-to-wall carpet, you won't get any paint or spatters on your rug.

If you line the bottom of your fireplace with heavy duty foil before making that fire, it will be ever so much easier to clean the ashes when that awful task comes knocking.

Also, if you sprinkle the dead ashes with water just before removing them, they won't make such a mess, either.

When you buy a roll of paper lining for your shelves, put it in an empty waxed paper or foil box. The serrated metal cutting edge tears off the paper beautifully.

You can cut those beautiful little plastic doilies and glue them to your bathroom or kitchen window to give you privacy. Your neighbor won't be able to see in, yet you can see out! Sometimes it takes the place of curtains.

And as for that kitchen windowsill which will invariably catch stuff and things and needs painting so often—why not put a piece of plastic wrap or adhesive-backed plastic on it? Great for the windows you keep your potted plants on, too.

Rubber rings on the bottom of potted plants will prevent rings.

Try putting a bottle cap or piece of sponge over that hole in the bottom and watch the soil stay inside instead of out.

What to do with that folded bedspread at night? Just open the top drawer of your chest of drawers and place the folded spread over it. Real handy.

If you ever want to "demoth" a closet or a bag full of out-of-season clothes, an easy way is to fill an old sock with some moth crystals and attach it with a rubber band over the end of the hose of your electric hair dryer.

Put the dryer on a closet shelf, close the door, and let it run ten minutes or so on COLD only—never heat.

A vacuum cleaner salesman told me that this same method could also be used in garment bags when storing out-of-season clothes.

Do you absolutely abhor making beds and running from one side to the other?

One gal who sleeps in a queen-sized bed scoots to the center of it before she gets out of the bed and with her legs wide apart, pulls the sheet (straightening and center-

ing it) up to her chin, then grabs the blanket (doing likewise) and last, the bedspread.

Before she gets out she bends her knees and gets a great big puff of air under them all. While lowering her legs, she pulls all the covers up over her chin. Gently slips out of the bed and it's practically made in full!

I've been doing this for three years and find it the greatest. At least that is one way to get a bit of exercise and it is quite an eye opener.

It's a snap, folks. I promise. Your bed doesn't have to be king- or queen-size to use this method. Try it on any kind.

If you don't have top sheets that are contoured at the bottom—try tying a knot at the bottom of those top sheets on each corner and tucking the excess under the mattress. Then when you jerk that top sheet up when making the bed, it won't slip.

These knots are easily untied for laundering.

For those who have electric blankets: Always turn them on thirty minutes before you go to bed. This will warm up the bed so you won't be jumping in an ice-cold winterland.

You can also put your pajamas and nightgowns between the sheets, and they are cozy and warm when you're ready to change.

If you have a baby in diapers and change him during the night, it is also nice to keep a few diapers and a nightgown or PJ's on top of the electric blanket, too. To replace that wet, cold diaper with a nice warm one is something junior will always love you for. He'll go back to sleep quicker, too.

And for those bottom-fitted sheets: These are really lulus when trying to put 'em on, eh? Especially if you have extra heavy mattresses.

Did you know that if you would put diagonal corners (one *top* corner first and then the bottom corner on the other side of the bed) on first, then continue, that they go on with half the effort? More of that hard-earned energy saved!

The greatest thing to stuff throw pillows with is plastic bags from your cleaners. Just wad them up as you would paper. So fluffy and easy to care for. Great for making extra bed pillows for that unexpected company. (Free, too.)

And for those with king-sized beds—the use of queen-sized top sheets and blankets (90" x 120") saves several dollars at the time of purchase. Also, the sides do not hang down so far when a short spread and flounce are used. Why just throw away your hard-earned money?

About those plastic stack-type vegetable bins: These are great if there is a shortage of linen closets in your home; and they come in all colors. I use them in the bathroom for extra towels and washcloths. Did you know that they fit wonderfully under your washbasin?

You can stack them to face the front of the basin or use two stacks and face them back-to-back, leaving open space on each side where the contents aren't so noticeable. This will give a solid-looking surface when facing it from the front.

If your medicine cabinet has the kind of door that opens (not the sliding type), throw your bath towel over the opened mirror before you take that bath or shower.

Your mirror won't be steamed up when the towel is removed. Saves more time and wipe ups.

And one reader says:

"I finally hit on an easy way to wipe off bath fixtures, tubs, walls, and so on. I wait until after I take a hot shower, when everything is covered with moisture.

"Then I take a soft cloth or paper towel and just wipe away. It's all clean and shiny in a jiffy and sure saves lots of energy!"

And for working folks who like and *should* hit the top when it comes to keeping an orderly house:

If you have to eat hamburger and beans for a week or two to pay for it—*do buy* yourself a carpet sweeper and a feather duster. I won't say they take the place of elbow grease and energy, but they really suffice. I wouldn't do without either of mine.

Both are the greatest for quickie jobs. There are always those days when we just don't have that energy, and emergencies do arise, you know. This wisp of top cleaning to get the effect of a clean house will calm our nerves. In a jiffy, you can carpet sweep the center of your rug and swipe at the dust on your tables with the feather duster. Then take a deep breath and get rid of that disgust at least. . . .

If you cut the corners off the sponge that is no longer clean enough to use in the kitchen sink, you can tell the "floor swiper" from the "dish swisher!"

And plain old mayonnaise is fantastic for removing scratches on furniture. Rub some on with your finger, let set awhile, and wipe off with a soft cloth.

If the scratch is very deep, remove the meat from a walnut or pecan and break it in half; rub with the broken side. This does a terrific job.

Did you know that if you wet your sponge or cloth mop first in water, then wring it out before putting it in your wax, that it wouldn't waste so much wax? Makes the mop easier to wash, too.

To make your chrome shine, just put a little peanut butter on a paper towel and rub. Then wipe off the excess oil or peanut butter. This works on sinks, stoves, bathroom fixtures, etc.

Those plastic clothes bags that come from the cleaners make fine trash collecting bags. Just tie a secure knot at the end with the small hole that the hanger goes through.

They are ideal for collecting upstairs trash from the various wastebaskets up and down the stairs; the bags are disposable and free.

Just slip an old woolen sock over your hand with the top side on your palm to dust all those tricky little places such as chair rungs, etc.

If you will put a coat or two of self-polishing wax on the walls of your bathroom tile—around your sink, tub and shower, it sure will prevent that water spotting. (Do *not* use on shower floors—it could cause someone to slip.)

I just finished wiping up my kitchen floor. While I was doing it, I wondered if anyone else used the kind of "mop rag" that I do. I think I've tried them all—string mops, sponge mops, old socks, and even old underwear. But I have yet to find one that does the job like one of your old nylon sweaters!

Like so many good things, I discovered this quite by accident when a torn nylon sweater was the only "rag" I could find.

Believe it or not, I used that sweater as a mop for two years before I changed it for another one—nylon again, of course. I have even used it on the cement floor of the utility room.

It soaks up water or any liquid quickly, and dries quickly, too. It has no time to get a musty smell, even if I forget to rinse it out, which has happened on several occasions.

### ❦ Pretty Up Your Office

This is for those of you who have typewriters (portable sewing machines, or any other type of heavy equipment, such as standard electric mixers): You know those legs with all the synthetic rubber on the bottom? Some of these leave marks on your desk, so why don't you do as I did last year?

Cut little pieces of carpeting, about the size of the gadgets on the bottoms of the legs, and glue them onto the rubber things—with the carpet side toward the furniture it's going to sit on! Fantastic!

Any kind of machinery will slide and glide over that beautiful surface, without leaving any scratches or rubber marks.

But, if you don't have any little pieces of carpet left over from something, you can get what they call scraps at most rug dealers. Usually they are free, or will cost only a few cents.


Here's another trick I learned recently when I had a few inches of carpeting left over from a patching job:

Thin, inexpensive carpet pieces can be glued to the bottom of lamps, heavy ash trays, vases (or just about any thing you want to glue it to,) and will prevent scratches on furniture. So save those tiny squares of carpeting and put them to good use.


Take a little time to work on projects that can make your office homey and cheerful. For instance, take your loved ones to work:

"I had a small clock that couldn't be fixed. I made a beautiful paperweight from it by taking off the front, very carefully removing the hands and placing a snapshot of my children inside.

"I used the glass front for a pattern to cut the picture the right size."

And since some of you have to live with those office desks eight hours a day, you might as well keep them nice.

Do this to your telephone pad: "Go over the alphabet on the outside of the telephone flip pads with colorless nail polish. This will protect the tabs too.

"It will not turn yellow like tape will. Works wonders."

And when you're called on to make a poster: "Use those felt ink markers and write on foil. We unrolled foil from the box, laid it flat on a table and printed away like mad.

"We did find that red and black markers make the most attractive signs. And we also learned that the marking did not smear when it rained as it did on our cardboard signs."

### Planting Tricks

Why not brighten up a dreary office with some plants?

"To make plants that grow in water look more attrac-

tive, put a few drops of blue and green food coloring in a huge snifter (or any clear glass container). Fill with water and add plants.

"Sure makes green plants look different in that lovely sea-green water!"

"To prevent spilling water when watering all those house—and office—plants growing in soil, I place ice cubes on top of the soil. Since the cube melts slowly, the ice does not shock the roots of the plant."

# ❦ Centerpieces With Wow!

Having a dinner party? Create such a smashing centerpiece that your guests even forget the food.

So many of us are always looking for a pretty centerpiece when having company for dinner, especially when we eat on the patio, balcony, or out in the backyard. I was in just such a predicament recently, so I thought I should share a trick that I thought of!

I happened to have a fresh pineapple. I twisted some of the narrow leaves out of the center, leaving a small hole. Then I cut off the outside leaves that were brown and dead-looking.

All there was to do then was to push a candle into the little hole in the top, light it, and use the pineapple itself as a centerpiece. It looked adorable on the table. Best of all, you can double your money's worth by cutting the pineapple up later and eating it.

"I keep a bunch of parsley in a little jar with a bit of water in my refrigerator, and it stays fresh for quite some time. (I also find that it deodorizes my refrigerator.)

"Parsley is good in an emergency for a centerpiece, arranged with lemons and other fruits, when you don't have a flower arrangement."

"To make artificial flowers really last a long time, or just to renew their appearance, I always coat the petals with clear or even pink fingernail polish.

"I have even used some frosted polish to paint some plastic geraniums, and the effect was very pleasing."

Use two or three colors of fingernail polish on those petals. Start at the bottom with the dark red and end up with lighter colors. I've found it most intriguing.

(And always remember when your flowers get so damaged you don't want 'em in the house, you can always stick them outside in your flower bed or wire 'em on a bush and fool your neighbors. I've been doing this for years.)

## A Green and Yellow Basket

Here's something absolutely fantabulous that I discovered quite by accident. You know those transparent, inexpensive, plastic wastebaskets we all buy? The kind that looks like cut glass? Usually you can get facial tissue boxes and the whole "caboodle" to match. Well, this weekend I needed a big container to plant a flower in. I picked up one of these wastebaskets, heated my icepick, and punched some holes in the bottom of it. But when I put the dirt in, it looked awful.

So I grabbed a can of black spray paint and sprayed the inside! You should see the beautiful results. It looks like a hand-carved piece of ebony! What a beautiful container for my potted plant!

Not only that, if your bathroom or bedroom is pink, green, or whatever, and you want to match your decor, try spraying the inside of the wastebasket with any color you need. I found flat paint to be the best.

They look so nice! This is a wonderful way to brighten up your office, too.

## ❦  All Lit Up

Some evening when you get ready to have a backyard party and you don't have permanent yard lighting (which is expensive), one of the cutest tricks I know is to use flashlights!

Borrow them from your neighbor if you have to. They add just the exotic effect you want, and at practically no cost.

I put flashlights under bushes and trees in such a way that they shine up and provide gorgeous indirect lighting. Another cute place to put them is in an urn, pot, or vase that is filled with artificial flowers or shrubbery! You'll be surprised at the lighting effect you get this way.

### 🐾 Your Garden of Earthly Delights

Spend your day off gardening. It's a wonderful change from the stuffy office, and good exercise too. You'll get results that you and your precious ones can really enjoy.

I don't know why it is, but it seems there is a little self-pride in all of us who plant our own gardens. We always try to beat our neighbor to the draw and have the first tomatoes, cucumbers, or radishes.

A lot of us plant our own seeds early, and grow them inside so we can set out our plants before they even come on the market. Growing seedlings and transplanting them sometimes runs into hard work. Besides, when transplanting there's always the danger of root shock.

Here is a real dilly I discovered quite by accident last year when I was trying to beat my neighbor to the harvest. I saved all my coffee cans with the plastic lids, cut out both ends of the cans and snapped the plastic lid back on the bottom.

As soon as I was sure my little seedlings were going to live, I transplanted them directly into this coffee can. After they got big, all I did was dampen the plant, tap the can to loosen the soil and then remove the plastic lid from the bottom. You can take your hand and push the clod of dirt right out the top! Isn't that wonderful? This way there is no root shock. These cans can be used over and over again during the season and from year to year.

I found, too, that you could just remove the plastic lid from the bottom and plant the whole caboodle (can, soil, and plant) in the ground, leaving about two inches of the coffee can sticking up above the earth. This not only kept the weeds out but as I watered each plant daily, it held the water.

Plants which have deep roots can grow through the hole in the bottom and grasp the earth that way.

Recently I learned a new method of pulling weeds that keeps your hands from getting stuck, cut, and covered with welts—especially on Johnson grass and stinging nettles (which hurt like the dickens if you touch them).

Take a plastic bag from the dry cleaners out to the yard with you. When you see some of those biting weeds, put the soft, thin bag over your hand, hold it around your wrist or elbow with the other hand and then just pull away!

You can work for hours in your garden with no marks or scratches on your arm, fingers, or hand. Also, since the plastic is thin and pliable, you can feel when the root is coming loose. How about that?

I have also used this method when cutting down sticky, thorny bushes. It's wonderful when you're trimming plants. Another thing—even though the weed is mushy after you have watered it, you don't get a bit of soil into the crevices of your hand or under your fingernails.

So let's go weed pickin'. But remember to take one of those plastic cleaner bags along with you. It's absolutely the greatest.

### ✨ Paint-a-thon
While you're out in the garden, take a look at that back porch! Bet it's just crying for a good paint job. Well, I've found a new way to paint an old wooden porch! This idea was born out of necessity because I couldn't find a paint brush.

This porch hadn't been painted in five years and the paint was off practically down to the wood. It was really in bad shape.

I happened to have one of those cheap synthetic sponges, so I just put on rubber gloves, dipped the sponge halfway into the well-stirred paint and started smearing. And smear I did!

Wowie! I could paint four times as fast. The paint-soaked sponge literally filled up all the nail holes and cracks, flowing into places where it was needed the most. (I found a brush didn't do this. It applies the paint too evenly.) And by coming back across the boards lightly as if I were using a brush, I didn't even make a brush stroke!

I don't advocate doing this while the sun is shining on your porch, because the lumber is hot and will dry the paint too fast.

And when it comes to painting under those steps and the sideboards—heavens to Betsy, you can do it in nothing flat with that good old sponge. I painted the whole porch in one-fourth the time it ordinarily would have taken me with a paint brush, and I feel I even did a better job.

If the paint is peeling on your porch or steps, be sure to use a wire brush and scrub it first before starting your paint job.

Or, if it's in too bad a condition, you can remove some of that peeling paint with ammonia and water. Just dilute it half and half with water and scrub down those steps or porch with your broom, then rinse with the garden hose. Be certain to let it dry *thoroughly*, because you can't paint over wet wood.

So give it a try. You won't even have a brush to clean. You can just throw that inexpensive old sponge away. And be sure to have an extra sponge and a pair of gloves handy that fit your husband. Who knows, he may decide to help you!

### ❦ Vacation Talk

What better way to spend a day off than recapturing your last vacation?

Many of us make home movies without a sound track, especially when we go on trips.

Recently, dear old friends of mine sent me a roll of movie film. While I was running the film a thought struck me: These friends have a tape recorder as well as a movie camera, so why not combine the two and have "talkies"!

If you're a home movie enthusiast and have a tape recorder, get out all your old movie reels and watch them by yourself.

As the film runs, tape-record where it was taken, who that person is, the fun you had on the trip and what is coming up next. It sure makes your movies more meaningful.

And as you replace the film in its box, put the tape away in a box, too, and store them together.

Now don't forget, the next time you take a movie film of your family, get that tape recorder out, plug it in and you can have live action and words at the same time.

You don't really have anything to lose because the tape can be used over and over again if it doesn't turn out satisfactorily. And it sure is fun to hear those voices when the movie is being run.

### ❦ Oven Reminders

Stop, look, and listen . . . And I mean just that.

Once in a while we all do stupid things. I just did—I was testing an oven cleaner in a fizz can (and believe me, I had read all of Joe Blow's instructions) and there was nothing on the can that said "Do not spray on the electric light in your oven!" Mine just exploded!

Thank goodness, I am "hard-of-seeing" and had my glasses on . . . (sometimes four eyes *are* better than two). A caution that some manufacturers have forgotten to remind us of is that nothing cold should be applied to a hot light bulb. Some directions say to heat your oven to 200 degrees. This makes the light bulb even hotter.

Whatever method you use to clean your oven, never touch the light bulb with a damp rag (this causes explosions, too, I found out) or spray it directly with anything cold.

## ☙ Wash Woodwork?

Everybody writes asking me how she should wash enamel woodwork. Heavens to Betsy—there are 50 million cleaners on the market! Each of us is different and has different kinds of wood and paints on the woodwork throughout our homes, but here's how I have done it for years:

Put about a gallon of warm water in a plastic wastebasket (or something!) and add a half cup of kerosene (bought at most filling stations for about 20 to 25 cents a gallon).

The kerosene will float on top of that warm water.

Dip an old washcloth or piece of bath towel in this, wring it out, and rub away.

I have been told by painters that this cannot hurt woodwork that is painted with enamel. In fact, they say it helps preserve it. Now, why didn't they tell us this years ago?

Anyway, this does not have to be rinsed, just wiped with a dry cloth, and leaves a glossy coat on your woodwork and doors (especially where handprints are left). It's also wonderful on painted metal cabinets in your kitchen. Wow, does it ever take off that greasy stuff!

Remember, don't try to use this with a sponge. Just use that old washcloth, towel, or piece of your husband's discarded T-shirt. Works like magic. Less effort, no paint taken off, and it leaves a glorious shiny surface.

Here's to the gals who use thin plastic gloves (or rubber household gloves, for that matter): I suggest dusting a little talcum or bath powder in the gloves before putting them on. They go on easily.

Also, talcum is great for making girdles slide on like magic! Either dust the inside of the girdle or yourself before pulling it on.

### ❦ Defrost Refrigerator

"I work in an apartment hotel and must defrost the ice unit in many refrigerators each week. Here is the best way to do it that I have run across in over twenty years:

"I take the biggest plastic wastebasket I can find and put it right in front of the refrigerator when I open the door and start defrosting. "I lay newspapers over all the food on the top shelf, being sure that the newspaper fits up against the wall of the refrigerator.

"The newspaper will catch any drips from the melting ice and keep it off the shelves below. Besides, if a big piece of ice falls off, then all I have to do is plop it into the wastebasket.

"I always leave the drip-tray under the frozen food compartment to catch most of the melted ice and water. I put newspapers on the linoleum in front of the refrigerator. They catch all the drippings and mess, and I don't have to clean the floor later.

"I *never* try to clean the entire refrigerator in one day.

I do the defrosting one day and clean the shelves another."

"Before starting to defrost a refrigerator or home freezer, I always put a pair of my husband's clean, old socks on my hands. This prevents my hands from touching the ice which always makes them sting and get numb."

"I live in an efficiency apartment. Everyone in the building has a problem defrosting the refrigerator. What a job this is!

"Our main trouble is emptying the tray beneath the freezer compartment when it fills up with water. What a mess this is to empty! It always spills.

"We finally discovered the answer: Don't empty it!

"Just turn the refrigerator back on, and let the water form into a solid brick of ice. Then put the ice in the shower stall or bathtub and let this melt. Or, just wait until it gets a thin film of ice on top, remove the tray, carry to the kitchen sink, and dump away.

"That's all there is to it! Sure saves mopping up the kitchen floor."

Here's a little dilly I figured out, and after experimenting with it, found it works like a charm:

Take any clean, old nylon stocking and stuff a sponge down into it—along the knee part. Tie two knots, one at each end of the sponge. Use your scissors to cut off each end. Or, instead of tying knots in the stocking, cut it off near each end of the sponge, miter it, and use safety pins to fasten it at each end.

Make at least three of these while you are at it. Put one in your kitchen to use for dishes. The sponge holds the water and suds and picks up the drips that nylon alone won't do.

Put another in your bathroom. Use this to bathe with!

Fantabulous. Oh—just wait until you try it. Also washes the tub like the genie from Aladdin's Lamp.

Put another in the trunk of your car. That "thing" will be mighty fine when the day comes to wash your car.

And, if you have the sponge and an extra stocking, why not make one for washing your windows? That little thing-a-ma-jig is worth its weight in gold when used for this purpose. But anyhow, do try one. You don't have a thing to lose—not even one penny, and this-kind-of-idea is the best.

# Chapter 5

# ✿ Dressed to Earn

Not only do we working gals have less time to spend on our outfits, but it's more important that we look just right.

While your little ones don't care a bit whether you're held together by a safety pin or by a few stitches, and hubby thinks your worn-out handbag is a good way to save money, your boss will wonder whether a gal who can't keep herself in good shape can keep his office in order!

But while you can't get away with downright sloppiness, a little trickiness will go a long way.

"For those who have difficulty with stubborn metal zippers, don't forget the old standby—an ordinary graphite pencil. Just rub it up and down the zipper. Then dust off the excess graphite dust, and sure enough an old zipper works like new.

"Of course, use it only on *dark* clothes."

Dressing in a hurry, and all your clothes have a mothball odor?

"For those musty mothball odors in clothes, try putting the garments in the clothes dryer and letting them tumble for five or ten minutes. They will come out like they've been freshly laundered or cleaned."

Ever dashed out of the office or a restaurant—with someone else's coat?

"Pin a small card or envelope addressed to yourself (with your phone number) inside your coat pocket. You can quickly determine which coat is yours, and someone else getting your coat by mistake will know you are the owner."

Have to cope with a crowded office closet? "Often the sleeves of my coat become wrinkled after hanging in a crowded closet.

"I solved this problem by rolling a rather thick section of newspaper fairly tight, shoving it up into each coat sleeve and then letting it expand, filling out the sleeves."

Sweater sleeves that are loose from being pushed up to the elbow can be tightened again by simply tying a knot in each sleeve end. Overnight is good, but leaving them a few days is even better.

If you will put iron-on tape on the *inside* of uniforms where medals and pins go, it will prevent tears and keep the fabric from drooping from the weight of the pin. It's dandy on nurses', volunteer helpers', Brownies' and Scouts' uniforms.

Glue one of those little name labels on a spring-type

clothespin. When removing your overshoes, snap the pin to them, thus identifying yours.

If the rear of your knit suit gets rump-sprung, put it on your ironing board, and spray the seat with water from a plunger-type bottle. Pat back in place and leave overnight to dry. Some gals turn the skirt wrongside out and use spray starch for this bottom job.

One can also use any large suitcase to store out-of-season clothes. Since they are rarely used, it's a great way to save on closet space.

"I've lost many head scarves by sticking them into my raincoat pocket (or any pocket for that matter) when I take my coat off.

"Know what I did? Using a razor blade, I undid the stitching on the top and the bottom of all the labels in the back of my coats. Now when I take off a scarf I use my finger to push the end of it through the label.

"I haven't lost one in over a year now."

I have been testing do-it-yourself dry cleaning machines, and I think they are wonderful. But have you ever thought of dry-cleaning your cotton garments in them?

Those blouses we use for everyday, or children's clothing with spots that will not come out when we launder them at home—can all be dumped into one of these fabulous machines. The cleaning fluid used in these machines will remove spots and soil marks that you and I cannot possibly get out in our home laundry machines.

But the greatest thing I found out was that I had less ironing to do! Nearly every one of my beautiful drip-drys did not even require a touch-up job with my iron.

The trick is to take your own hangers. When that machine stops, take out the garments *immediately*, fluff them in the air, shake 'em a little, and hang them up on those coat hangers.

And I suggest that you don't use plastic coat hangers for this. Metal ones are the best—preferably the type that are covered with tissue.

While you are at it, why not add a few of your husband's ties (the ones with gravy stains), or a few of your good linen dinner napkins that have lipstick and butter stains on them that you can never really get clean. The dry-cleaning solvent will remove most of the stains that you are unlikely to remove at home.

### ✌ Your "Bread" Bag

If you happen to be lucky enough to have one of those beautiful leather-lined purses, here's a tip for storing: Don't close it when storing it for a long time. Always stuff it full of crumpled newspapers and leave the top or fastener open. This will help eliminate mildew because the paper absorbs the moisture.

These beautiful purses cost so much we should take care of them.

"When I buy a straw purse that also has a straw handle, I always paint the handle with clear fingernail polish. You will be amazed how much longer the handle will last, and it doesn't get soiled so quickly."

"I found a dandy use for clear adhesive-backed plastic paper: I put some in the bottom of my white purse.

"Besides keeping the bottom of the purse clean, the plastic saves wear and tear on my bag."

"I put my house key on a shoelace and tie it to the zipper ring inside my purse. I just feel for the shoelace and there is my key—no groping or dumping out my purse trying to find it."

## Jewels for the Jewels

"An adhesive-backed bandage applied to the underside of a lapel or the inside of a dress, where a heavy brooch or pin is to be worn, will keep such a pin from being lost.

"Pin through the material and the bandage, lock the little safety catch, and forget it. It can't slip out."

Let's make a splash—go dump your costume jewelry drawer on the kitchen table.

Pick out your favorite pieces and put them back in the drawer. The pieces you haven't worn in ages just leave on the table. I'll bet you a buffalo nickel you'll end up with half of what's been in that drawer for the last ten years.

I just did this and you'd be surprised what I got rid of. Some of it was too good to throw away. So my teen-age daughter, one of her friends, and a neighbor, picked out pieces they liked.

Now the girls at the office, as well as your neighbors, probably have some jewelry, too, that is just cluttering up their drawers. So why not trade? Always remember that one person's "castoffs" may be another's gold mine. That's why they put ads in the paper and have garage sales.

## ❦ Scents-Appeal

From a working gal who should know: "I sell perfume and quite agree that all of those beautiful bottles of perfume and cologne should be displayed proudly.

"But please, ladies, do not display them where they will be in the sun. Your perfume will actually change and over a period of time the fragrance will evaporate!"

Another good idea: "I never throw away any empty perfume bottles. After all the perfume is gone, I discard the top and put the bottle in a drawer, or clothes closet. The minute amount of aroma that escapes slowly is heavenly."

(Empty perfume bottles are also good to put in the bottom of a clothes hamper, particularly if you do your laundry only once a week.)

And since perfume is mostly alcohol, try pouring some rubbing alcohol into the empty bottle and shaking it up. It mixes like a charm. This can be used for massages and is especially wonderful for the bedridden.

Now you men don't dare read another line! This hint is just for us women. You all know those fabulous new rubber-type filled, supported, or partial bras we are buying now? Here are some *dont's:*

Don't bleach 'em.

Don't boil them in dye remover or strippers of any sort.

Don't soak them in strong solutions overnight.

And *never* put them in a dryer.

All of these things *ruin* this type of bra and will deteriorate the foam padding inside. There is no way to remove and replace this quilted or stitched padding. I know. I tried!

When I was trying to purchase another bra, I asked the clerk if the white would stay white or if it would turn yellow in a few months. She didn't know.

I spied an ecru-colored one (this is a sort of beige), and an idea was born. Why not buy some ecru all-purpose dye at any dime store and tint any discolored bras?

That I did. Not only do they look quite presentable now, but here's something else I found out. Because the bra is sort of flesh-colored, when you put your slip over it, you do not see those white straps showing through thin clothes!

So don't forget, ladies: Don't throw 'em away, don't ruin 'em; just tint 'em.

I used to have a problem with those long-line bras with the wide boning. The boning would always come through the bra before I had a chance to wear it very long.

I found a solution! Trot right down to the drug or dime store and buy some moleskin plasters that are ordinarily used for corns. It's not a brand name—it's a type of thick padding with adhesive on one side.

Cut the size you want (I cut mine about the size of a nickel) and stick this to the inside of your bra where it hurts.

If you use this method *before* the bra gets a hole in it, you most likely will prevent the hole. The thing I like about it best is that it keeps from making another hole in my *skin!*

"I found a way to fasten my brassiere without straining my arm and shoulder. I just turn my brassiere around and fasten it in front where I can see what I am doing. Then I pull it around so the fasteners are in back, put my arms through the straps, and pull them up.

"Presto, no strain and it's quick and easy."

Many of you gals have asked how to launder bras and other garments containing spandex fabric without their turning yellow and deteriorating. I wrote to Miss Edna Schappert of the Man-made Fiber Producer's Association, and she has come to our rescue with the following information:

"When laundering undergarments containing spandex, do not use a chlorine-based bleach or a detergent containing chlorine bleach. Chlorine will weaken and discolor the spandex fibers. Instead, a detergent containing no chlorine, and a perborate-based or oxone-based bleach *may* be used.

"Labels on bleach containers will indicate if the product is chlorine-based, perborate-based, or oxone-based. Labels on detergent containers will indicate if chlorine is contained in the detergent.

"Heavily soiled areas in garments containing spandex may be pretreated by thoroughly rubbing those areas with a thick paste of water and detergent or soap. Then allow the garments to soak for a period of time.

"When machine-washing undergarments containing spandex fibers, use the 'low' temperature setting. It is advisable to *air-dry* (rather than machine-dry) garments containing spandex fibers. It is also important to follow special instructions on manufacturers' hangtags and labels in caring for garments containing spandex fibers."

Miss Schappert deserves a standing ovation for this valuable information! I highly recommend that these spandex garments be washed daily. The body oils from our skin, when embedded in the fiber, can also do lots of damage.

## ✧ The Killer

If you *must* wear a girdle—and I realize many of you working ladies have to—you really should learn how to care for them. For instance, do you know how much perspiration they absorb? They will last so much longer if thrown in the washer frequently with the bath towels.

Remember, nine times out of ten, any girdle you buy is a man-made fabric. It has no pores! Your towel will scrub against this "hold-in" project and it will last longer. Don't let perspiration rot those fabulous girdles. I've learned from an authority that the rubbing action in washing makes them last far longer than if we allow the soil and perspiration to build up.

To make the hurdle with the girdle a bit easier, try this:

"My hint won't help you get your work done, but it may stop a temper next time you try to put on your girdle! I've found that by putting on my stockings *first,* the girdle slides on much easier.

"When I get the top of the girdle to about hip level, I fasten the stockings without a lot of pulling or twisting, then just pull the girdle the rest of the way up smoothly and evenly."

## ✧ Don't Be Slipshod

A friend of mine once bought a beautiful nylon slip with gorgeous lace on top, but made the mistake of wearing it with a navy blue knit suit that faded. She couldn't get the stains off the slip, even with pure bleach.

If this ever happens to you, grab a wash cloth and pour lots of rubbing alcohol on it. Rub the stained portion between folds of the alcohol-soaked rag. Don't ask me why, but this works!

### Are You Slipping?

"To keep your slip straps from showing when wearing a boat-shaped neckline, pin a tiny safety pin in each shoulder seam—taking care that it doesn't come through on the right side of the material.

"Slide your strap through the pin and snap it shut. This will allow the straps to give as you move. The pins are easily removed for washing or cleaning the dress."

"Paper clips are absolutely ideal for keeping bra and slip straps together. They are so easy to use, and much better than safety pins, especially if you wear bifocals."

### Beating the Clinger

"I have a real silk dress that clings to me, especially in cold weather. I tried taffeta and cotton slips and petticoats, but still it would cling. Finally I made a half-slip of your famous nylon net using a gored skirt pattern, and that solved all my problems.

"I wear the nylon net half-slip over my other slip, and this takes up very little room."

This works because the holes in the net let air through.

"I have several partially lined slim skirts and often wear half-slips with them. I used to spend half my time adjusting and smoothing. I usually step into my skirts and the slip wants to 'ride up.'

"I discovered that if I placed the half-slip inside the skirt, stepped into both at the same time and then pulled them up—everything was straight, smooth, and comfortable."

If your synthetic fabric garments cling to you because of static electricity—here is the solution, again from Miss

Edna Schappert of the Man-made Fiber Producer's Association:

"Static is the force which causes the attraction of small bits or particles to an object after the object has been rubbed or exposed to abrasion. Sometimes in cold, dry weather, garments made from man-made fibers have a tendency to cling to the body, and this clinging is caused by what is commonly called static.

"This clinging tendency can be reduced in washable garments by adding a small amount of liquid detergent, fabric softener, or a special liquid anti-static agent to the final rinse water. Liquid anti-static agents can be obtained at notion counters in drug or department stores. Care and handling directions on labels and hangtags should, of course, be followed."

### ❦ No Spots, No Lint

Yes, spotless is how you can appear on the job. And would you believe that a foam rubber curler in your desk or handbag is part of your ammunition?

"I find that one of my large foam rubber curlers is very effective in removing lint and hairs from my clothes. In fact, it's so quick I prefer it to brushing. Since they are small they can easily be carried in a handbag."

A nylon sock helps, too! "The nylon sock leaves no lint to be brushed from the cleaned garment, as when using a cloth."

Just what the doctor ordered is this hint: "I taught nursing for years and many times have told the students to rub straight baking soda on the outside of their white uniform's underarms. It's a wonderful, inexpensive deodorizer."

You can also use a powder puff and dust the baking soda under your arms like talcum powder.

One of my dearest friends told me that she puts a nylon half-slip over her head, letting the elastic come under her chin, to keep make up off her dresses when putting them on or taking 'em off.

I tried it, by golly, and it does work! Not only does this protect your lips but your make up and your hairdo as well!

## ❦ Wrapped in Plastic

Here's a little hint for those of you who wear white dresses and want to save on cleaning bills. When you are going out, grab a plastic cleaning bag and put it on the car seat *before* you sit down.

Remember, those cushions may not be clean. When you stop and think about it, I don't suppose any of us clean them very often, do we? This is also a wonderful idea for those who dress in fragile formals. If your gown is long, put a plastic bag on the floor of the car. This keeps your hem from getting soiled. (Don't forget to use caution though, and keep these bags out of the reach of children and pets.)

This clever lady goes even further:

"One evening we were going to a formal party given by my company for all employees. The taxi was waiting and it was pouring.

"I quickly cut off both shoulder corners of a dry cleaner's plastic bag so my feet would go through, opened the big end putting my feet through the holes I had cut and drew it up to my waist!

"Got to the hotel, stepped out of the bag, my husband rolled it up and put it in his topcoat pocket. Not a spot on my gown!"

## ❦ Wool Gathering

For years I've been washing, drying, and stretching sweaters. I've used every idea, and tried to figure out how to eliminate that crease across the shoulders which I think is unsightly. Read on, gals!

After washing and then rinsing a sweater in vinegar water (this takes any odor out), I squeezed it thoroughly. Don't wring it or twist it. Then I threw it up in the air about ten times and caught it with my hands each time.

This allows the air to get back in the knit, brings back the original shape, and spreads what little moisture is left among the fibers—which is good. And *most* important I then took my broom and literally threaded the sweater on its handle, through one sleeve, past the neck, and out the other sleeve! This funny looking "scarecrow" I put *across* my clotheslines.

Since then I have learned that I can cut off a broom or an old mop handle, stack 'em up in a corner and use 'em for drying many things—quilted housecoats, babies' padded jackets, drip-dry shirts, etc.

Gals, this way they dry with *no* crease at all. And dry quicker because air gets inside.

Cane fishing poles are also marvelous for this, because you can hang more than one garment on the same pole. And you don't have to cut the mop or broom off the end, either. Sometimes I just use mine as is.


One angel wrote: "This is how I remedy snags in my sweaters. I push the head of a straight pin through the wrong side of the knit, wrap the snag around the pin head and then pull it through to the wrong side again.

"This has worked everytime for me, and the snags can no longer be seen."


"Try hanging drip-dry blouses upside down to dry. It's the collar you want the weight of the water to smooth out, not the tail of the blouse."

"Here's an idea for those who wear wool turtleneck sweaters and are bothered by the scratchy feeling and an itchy neck. Cut the *top* four inches off a nylon stocking, slip it over your head and around your neck under the sweater.

"Your problem is solved. No scratching at all."

### 💇 Travel Right

Whether your trip is business or pleasure, these packing tips are bound to please:

"When I pack a suitcase, instead of folding my clothes, I lay them flat on the bed and cover them with a full plastic bag. Then they can either be rolled or folded for the

trip. I find they are not wrinkled when I arrive at my destination."

She's right. I tried this myself. It seems that the litttle bit of air which is trapped in the plastic bag prevents wrinkles!

Since your dress or suit usually comes back from the cleaner in a plastic bag and on a wire coat hanger, *don't* remove them when packing. Fold the garments into your suitcase—plastic bag, hanger, and all! Then when you get to your destination, all you have to do is hang them up.

One more thing. Have you ever noticed how we usually take too many clothes on a trip? Well, since the clothes won't wrinkle in the plastic bags, anything you don't wear can be put back in your closet at home without pressing!

## ☙ Sew Perfect

A hundred years ago when I took sewing in high school, they made me baste every seam in a garment. The following generation, including my daughter, learned to pin everything.

Did you ever start to sew and couldn't find a straight pin in the house? Well, it happened to me. Even with trying to locate all the safety pins, corsage pins, and hat pins, it still wasn't enough.

While going through the bathroom drawer trying to locate a few more, I spied those metal hair clips we pin our hair up with! They are terrific to use instead of the old-fashioned straight pins for basting. It's an especially good idea to use them on satin or any fragile material where a pin hole would show. It also saves the time of pushing the pins through the material twice and pulling 'em out again!

# Chapter 6

# ❦ My Secret Love

It's nylon net!

Probably the most useful item you gals will ever find. From cleaning to cooking to dressing, it's just what the busy—and economical—woman needs. Let your men laugh—until they, too, find out what a long way a piece of this miracle-cloth goes:

"Every spring my husband and I drain our fish pond, clean it out, and scrape off the sides after the slime has been hosed off.

"This year while he was trying to scrape off the film with a wire brush, I calmly walked in the house and got a ball of your nylon net and proceeded to wipe the film off in *nothing flat!*

"He asked what in the world I was using. So I just handed him another ball of net and we cleaned the fish pond in short order.

"He said maybe I had better buy some more net and keep it on hand for another job. I nearly fell over laughing and replied, 'That's exactly what Heloise recommends.'"

Men are not the only ones snared by nylon net:
"Nylon net scrubbers are perfect toys for wee babies.
"They are easily kept clean and fresh, are lightweight, can be dropped, thrown, 'scrunched,' or whatever, and best of all, are most economical for all of us on budgets!"

"When drying crocheted or flannel baby bootees, a small ball of net placed in each bootee not only allows the air to circulate for faster drying, but helps to keep the bootees from drying out of shape."

"Cover a soap-filled, steel wool pad with about four layers of nylon net. Make a circle of the net larger than the pad, and just gather it with heavy thread, string, or a rubber band. It's perfect to stick diaper pins into—keeps them so shiny and sharp."

"We love nylon net pompons at our house. They are good not only for scrubbing dishes, but also washcloths for scrubbing children.
"I make miniature pompons for my older daughter to use as complexion brushes."

And older people find it just as fantabulous:
"I use your nylon net instead of straw or cut-up cellophane to line my Easter baskets.
"No mess now when the basket spills. Also, a big net bow on the handle of the basket looks terrific."

And good for your bird cages:
"I tie a double piece of nylon net about three-quarters of

the way up and round the outside of my messy Myna bird's cage. "He used to get food all over the floor. But this way while he can see out and we can see in, the net keeps his food in the cage."

Fantastic for furniture:
"Recently we purchased a lovely new sofa-and-chair set. I felt that the back and arms should be protected some way. Your famous nylon net came to my rescue.

"I bought it in colors that matched the sofa. Then doubled it and put it over the back and arms of the furniture where they get the most soiled.

"Worked well as a protector and was hardly visible. But best of all, those pieces can be removed and washed easily."

"A sponge wrapped in nylon net is excellent for cleaning upholstery when used with a good, recommended upholstery shampoo. (And the greatest for doing dishes and bathing!)

"I learned from a hotel keeper that whether you buy the sponges already covered, or cover them yourself, they do a great job, and are far better than expensive brushes formerly used for this purpose."

Ladies, you can even wear it:
"To avoid wear in the elbows of your sweater sleeves, baste pieces of nylon to the inside of the sleeves (at the elbows). These will usually last the life of the sweater."

It cleans your clothes:
"When my son left for college, I wondered how he was going to get rid of the light colored lint that collects on his black suit, topcoat, and dark pants.

"I measured the inside coat pocket, then folded several thicknesses of black nylon net to the right size, bound it with black tape, and put it in his pocket.

"He says it works wonderfully, and because of the color he has managed to use it in public without anyone noticing."

And helps keep them fresh:
"With nylon net, you can make wonderful bags for moth crystals to thumbtack in your closet or wardrobe. Hang these near the top of the closet. The fumes will go downward and leave a fresh, protective odor."

Nylon net for dishwashing:
"That ever faithful nylon net stretched over the middle prongs of the top tray in my dishwasher keeps small particles from falling through. I leave mine on all the time, and the heating element doesn't affect it at all."

"I lined the flatware section of my dish drainer with some of your nylon net, using basting stitches to hold it to the drainer. Now I never lose any small items (such as the screws of the meat grinder) when I wash dishes."

### ❦ Nylon Net on Hairbrush
Let me give you a tip, and don't laugh until you try it.

Hairs are extremely hard to pull out of a hairbrush. We break many combs trying to remove them. Nylon net can be bought at most fabric and department stores for less than forty cents a yard. Buy six inches of this! This will cost you less than seven cents! Besides, you will have some left over.

Take the six-inch width of nylon net and cut off a piece three times the length of your hairbrush. Fold the net from the handle over the brush part and back to the handle again, taking the little extra swatch left and wrapping it around the handle a few times. Then brush your hair!

The nylon net will sink down into the hairbrush but . . . the loose hairs will never get down into the bottom of the brush again, and your hair will stay cleaner between shampoos.

After brushing your hair with this, untwist the net, hold it over the wastebasket, and drop the hairs into that old wastebasket.

Give it a whirl, gals. I am positive that you will love it and never use a hairbrush again without first covering the bristles with nylon net.

As a gift, I received one of those wonderful, specially-treated, no-grease-necessary skillets, and I was afraid to use it because I might ruin the finish when I cleaned it! I told my next-door neighbor about it, and can you guess what she said to use on it? Yes, it's your nylon net to the rescue again!

My neighbor uses her nylon net scrubber on her treated pans all the time. There isn't the tiniest scratch on them, yet it is abrasive enough to wipe off any remaining food.

Also for salads:

"When I make egg salad sandwiches, salads, deviled eggs, or the like, instead of using a grater to prepare my hard-boiled eggs, I use a piece of nylon net. It really saves time. I cut my eggs in half and put a half in the middle of the net and twist as you would twist the top of a bag. The egg squeezes easily through, ready for use.

"Shake the nylon net in clear water and it can be reused many, many times."

When I first heard this idea, I thought surely the egg

couldn't squeeze through the net. The yolk maybe, but not the white. Wouldn't the net split? I went out to the kitchen and boiled six eggs. I cut one in half and tried this hint. I could hardly believe my eyes—the most beautiful shredded eggs you ever saw dropped into my bowl, white and all!

I deviled the remaining five eggs by shredding the yolks the same way. I ended up having twice as much filling to stuff my egg with. They were beautiful, light, and "un-lumpy." So don't hesitate to prepare grated eggs the nylon net way. You won't even have a grater to wash!

Take it on a picnic:

"I always take along a three-yard piece of wide nylon net when we go on a picnic and use it to cover containers of food.

"It keeps flies and other insects off the food, and those going back for seconds can see through the net and pick out the food they wish."

Use it to make a hamburger:

"To make a thick or thin hamburger, put a ball of ground beef between two layers of net and just press!

"It doesn't stick to the net and comes out any thickness you desire. The net washes beautifully and it also keeps the sticky goo off your hands when pressing the hamburger meat."

And after you've cooked with it, clean with it too:

"How often I used to struggle to clean flour from my corrugated meat pounder—until I used nylon net. It quickly swished off the goo.

"A piece of nylon net is wonderful to clean the dough board or table after making pie crust or bread. Let the net dry and wipe it clean. Running water from the faucet will clean the net.

"Now the dishcloth will not get sticky when you wash the table or dough board during that final clean-up job."

"We made a pad of your fabulous nylon net, and it is wonderful for scooting crumbs off the cookie sheet when we are ready to bake another batch."

It's good for ovens:

"Another use for nylon net is for cleaning oven grates. It folds nicely around the rungs and doesn't fall apart before the job is done."

Good for floors:
"I use nylon net to scrub my floors when I'm stripping off the old wax. Just soak the floor for a while with a good commercial wax remover, then scrub away.
"Lots easier on the hands than steel wool."

Scrub with it:
"When doing wash by hand, I find nylon net perfect for scrubbing soiled spots such as neckbands on shirts and blouses. It works like the old-fashioned scrub board, but is so gentle on the fabric."

"I got a 12-inch square of nylon net, wadded up another piece about the same size and put it in the center of the first. I enclosed scraps of bath soap and fastened the net shut with a rubber band.

"I keep this scrubber in my laundry room to scrub shirt collars and cuffs, and dirty spots on garments before putting them into the washing machine."

Get rid of the bugs with it:

"Upon returning from an extended trip, we found that our car headlights and grill were spotted with dead bugs and accumulated dirt. After trying 'elbow grease' and detergent, I thought of using a little detergent and nylon net.

"Believe me, our headlights looked like Aladdin's lamps."

By all means clean your boat with it:

"Did you know that nylon net works just fine for removing dirt, scum, etc., from the bottom and sides of a fiberglass boat?

"I usually wipe off our boat while it's still in the water. After it's taken out, it only needs to be hosed off."

Everyone loves it, except the birds:

"To keep the birds out, spread a big piece of that wonderful nylon net over your strawberry (or any berry) bed in your garden and weigh the edges down with heavy rocks. The sun, rain, and water come through.

"It's inexpensive, does the trick, and will last many seasons."

# Chapter 7

# ❧ Odds and Ends

Most people don't have the time to learn how to balance meals.

So many of us are not home economists. We don't know one type of vitamin from another, and I am sure that most of us (me included) don't know exactly which foods contain exactly what vitamins. I have never seen this information on a can or box of frozen vegetables.

However, when you cook the main meal in your little domain, there *is* one way to balance your diet without getting out your adding machine and health book . . . and it takes no college degree.

Cook by color!

We usually have meat. As an example: This is usually "brownish" color. I do not consider meat a color when using this simple method. If it's fish . . . it's white and that's not a color either.

When we want to have a balanced diet at any meal, we must have at least two colors. Better yet . . . three or four.

If you have potatoes or rice, which are *white,* then you need something green and red.

When we say *green,* this could mean green cabbage, kale, peas, broccoli, lettuce, asparagus, spinach, green beans, or anything you happened to have on hand that is green . . .

Now, when we say something *red,* it doesn't mean that you have to have a fruit or vegetable that is actually red. So long as it comes from a family that is "attached" to red. It could even be orange. Take sliced (or canned) tomatoes, cooked (or raw) carrots, beets, cranberry sauce, tomato aspic, etc . . .

Another color is *yellow.* This could mean pineapple, which can be dressed up by topping a slice of it with grated cheese (orange!) and some wonderful mayonnaise (yellow!) and a little paprika for color. This makes a wonderful salad when placed on a lettuce (green!) leaf.

Another yellow example is hard-boiled eggs. We all need eggs. They can be cooked ahead of time and placed in our refrigerators and used for so many things.

Examples: When you have some leftover ham, bacon, dried beef or tuna fish (and my, are these wonderful fill-ins for the days when you are tired or in a hurry), chop up the meat and the whites of the hard-boiled eggs. Put these in some cream sauce and pour over a piece of toast. Then grate the yellow of the egg through a tea strainer and sprinkle it on top of the toast. Yellow again!

If all you have for salad is some lettuce . . . try buying an egg slicer (less than forty cents at your dime store), peel that hard-boiled egg, put it in your slicer and then lay the slivers across the top of that hunk of sliced or diced lettuce. I like mine shredded for a change. Beautiful . . . and really professional!

Top this with Thousand Island or French dressing, or mayonnaise. And don't forget the paprika. It's inexpensive and goes a long, long way. Makes it appetizing. Here again you have your colors. Vary your salad some days with peas, pickled beets or carrot sticks.

As long as you have any three colors, perferably four, on your dinner plate . . . then you are not going to be too far off when it comes to a balanced diet.

Learn to *mix* your colors for the dinner table. When you have meat and mashed potatoes, always serve something colorful with it. Add a dash of red, yellow, or green. I am of the opinion that every supper table should have something from the green and red "family" on it.

Color (for those like me who don't know or haven't the time to get books and study) is the answer to serving simple, balanced meals. Learn to cook by color and see with what relish your meals are eaten . . .

Never throw away one of those plastic ice foam chests. They are the greatest for sewing baskets. Put a cigar box in there for your scissors, bobbins, and spools, and use the top to stick your needles and pins in. Great for kiddie's toy chests too.

And have you ever put your sprinkling in it? Keeps it from drying out. Place a bag of ice in it if you can't get all your ironing done in one day.

Don't ever let anything sour or mildew if you just give up and can't finish those sprinkled pieces. Put 'em in a plastic bag and keep it in your refrigerator.

If you find that it will be a few days before you get around to the chore, put the bag in your deep freezer.

Your sprinkled clothes will last indefinitely that way. And the pieces are even easier to iron.

And if you have lots of ironing to do, wrap an old nylon stocking around that iron handle and pin it with a safety pin. Saves blisters and tired hands. The iron scoots along like an ice skater.

Old nylon stockings are wonderful, too, when tying up old newspapers and shrubbery for pick up day. They stretch . . .

And for those with poor vision who have thermostats in their home, just put a dab of red fingernail polish on the 75 degree mark. You can spot that bright red mark quickly and need only to push it slightly to the right or left to make it warmer or cooler.

Fluorescent tape which comes in rolls is great for many things. Cut a tiny circle out and put it on your doorbell button. Can be seen at night easily.

Put a piece of it on your garbage disposal switch and all hot water faucets. Also put tiny pieces on your favorite TV channels, the 350-degree mark on your oven, and on light switches so they can be easily seen at night. This tape can be bought at dime stores.

Use a plastic shower cap to cover seats on bicycles and tricycles. Really comes in handy when it rains. The elastic holds the cover in place, and the seat doesn't fade either.

For those who have balconies, patios, and porches and use redwood furniture—try turning it upside down and nailing a metal bottle cap on the bottom of each leg. Scoots like a slick whistle. The caps also keep the legs off the wet concrete in rainy weather.

When you open your newspaper, slit it down the middle before reading it, it's great for reading in bed since it's much easier to handle.

Paper doilies are good for something that they weren't ever intended for. Try gluing them to windows—especially the basement and attic windows. Looks like starched lace curtains.

If you have trouble with your purse sliding off the car seat while driving (very dangerous when trying to hit that brake fast), just hook it through your seat belt before you fasten it.

And when you put bags of groceries in the car seat, use that seat belt to fasten around the sack . . . especially if it's got eggs or milk cartons in it.

And for those who have dark dials on their stoves and ovens and the worn numbers are hard to see: Just mark over them with a child's white crayon and then rub the dial with a piece of paper towel and they will come out like new again.

Don't throw away that plastic dishpan when it springs

a leak. I use mine under the kitchen sink as a storage bin for soaps and waxes. The cleaning products are all in one place and I can just pull the pan out like a drawer.

I remove the discoloration from my aluminum pots and pans by boiling two tablespoons of cream of tartar in a quart of water for about twenty minutes. This works wonders. The darkness in aluminum is caused by minerals in the water.

I suggest that you take a soap-filled scouring pad and give the pan a once-over swab (not a hard cleaning) after using this method. These soap-filled pads contain a jewelers' rouge that makes the pot real shiny and you will love it.

To remove thick tomato paste from a can in nothing flat, open at *both* ends, scraping one end on the edge of the can as you remove it. With the other end still in place, just push the paste right through the can with two fingers. Nary a bit left.

When cooking pancakes, only oil the skillet the first time, then use a raw Irish potato cut in half to rub the skillet with. As the potato cooks, just cut off a thin slice and continue. No sticking and no grease.

*Odds and Ends* 111

And why put that dab of leftover pancake and waffle dough back in the refrigerator? Go ahead and cook the extra, except not quite as brown, and refrigerate them. Just pop 'em in your toaster next time you get a hunger pang for some. Saves both time and waste.

If you want to keep yourself cool in the summer and warm in the winter when sleepy time comes around, save those plastic rubbing alcohol and bleach bottles!

When it's cold, fill them with hot water from your faucet and tuck a few of them in your bed about thirty minutes before you crawl in.

When it's hot, fill them nine-tenths full of water and set them in your freezer compartment. An hour before you go to bed put iced bottles between the sheets. The price is just right, as neither cost you anything.

Plastic curtains bought at your dime store make lovely dust ruffles. And while you're at it, buy another matching set for your windows.

And when some casserole or pot pie drips on the floor of your oven and makes a terrible smell and smoke . . . just grab for that good old box of salt again and *pour* it on the spills quickly. Make this thick. The odor and smoke will stop immediately. The oven does not have to be turned off to do this. Just close the oven and continue your baking.

Now here's the trick to it all: When that salt has baked itself on (even if you bake a few more days), use your pancake turner and scoop it up. Cleaning is easy then.

Here's a little tip all homemakers should know:

When you put your cooking utensils on a shelf, always place the handle in first. This way you don't have to pull them all out to see which pot or pan you need.

When having slipcovers made, always buy additional material. When the slipcovers are dry cleaned or washed, do likewise with the extra piece. Then, when the arm rests become worn, they can be replaced with similar looking cloth, thereby extending the life of the slipcovers.

Here's an easy way to make those bathroom shag rugs look new again. After washing the rug, take a clean wire dog brush (any stiff pet brush will do) and brush it vigorously. This rids the rug of matting and tangles, and leaves it silky soft.

This method is also excellent for rejuvenating the fuzzy seat covers and tank covers that are so popular now. It's best to do this just before they're completely dry. If you have a dryer, put them back in for another ten minutes and watch them fluff up.

For the hard working gal who just hasn't too much energy left and wants to save what she can when it comes to cleaning the bathtub—go to the children's toy department and buy yourself a child's little toy wet mop. It's the perfect size to wet-and-wipe away with, and will save that tired back. Also good to get the spots off the tile wall over the tub.

And when you get a little spill on that kitchen or bathroom floor, why wet a big, old heavy mop? That tiny thing will do just as good a job.

In the morning when I open a can of frozen orange juice, I put it in my pitcher, add the water, and stir. But sometimes I find frozen lumps still there. I have now learned to use my potato masher! Just mash it and stir for a minute. It's all dissolved and ready to serve.

Safety includes letting the other person know what you are doing or intend to do. If your automobile is disabled on

our busy streets or highways, move it to the side of the street or onto the shoulder, if possible, and use flares, red flags, or other warning devices to let others know of your predicament.

If you do not have any special warning devices, the very minimum you can do is to raise the hood and trunk lid of the automobile to alert motorists approaching your car from either direction. To make this action even more effective at night, you may wish to paint the inside of the trunk lid with a fluorescent paint or apply strips of reflector tape.

"I am a retired florist and would like to give some tips to your housewives. Cut flowers last longer if all the leaves are removed from any stem that is under the water. The leaves sap up the power of life in a cut flower. The main point is to get to the bud itself.

"If you have no proper frog or foam, the extra leaves and sprigs may be tucked into the flower container. Often, sprigs of foliage with leaves still attached (such as stems from hedges) may be tucked down into a deep vase and used as a perfect flower arrangement.

"For some types of flowers, such as marigolds, a few drops of household bleach, added to the water before placing the flowers in, will help keep the stench down."

Rings from the top of metal beverage cans are the very thing to use for sewing into café curtains for the kitchen, bathroom, or the children's room. They are especially handy for people who like to make their own curtains.

For ball-point pens that just "don't" . . . One can often light a match and hold it on the very tip of the "ball," then scribble quickly on a piece of paper and nine times out of ten, it will write again . . . that is, if it's not out of ink! Watch it, if the pen is plastic be sure not to get the flame too close—you might melt it.

Now all of you who have those throw rugs, take heed! Broken hips and legs are not only expensive, but quite painful.

Did you know that you could take a plastic bag (such as comes on your garments from the cleaners), wrinkle it slightly and place it under your throw rug and it will help prevent slips? Works on asphalt tile, too.

Many people have a nosebleed or perhaps cut their hand and can't remove the stains from their clothing immediately. Well, I'd like to tell you about something I did recently when it happened to me.

I got a spot of blood on a white garment and did not notice it for about an hour. It was just about dry by that time! In fact, it probably was.

I picked up a small bottle of three percent hydrogen peroxide solution (which costs less than twenty cents at my drug store) and put a terry washcloth underneath the spot. Poured the peroxide on top of the spot and watched it foam away!

When I saw the blood dissolving, I took my fingernail and scratched the little bubbles, then poured more peroxide on the spot. Next I poured peroxide on a facial tissue and rubbed the top. When the blood started to sink into the terry washcloth, I used a clean cloth. Continued this and within two minutes, the spot was gone. Imagine that!

Be careful what you use this method on because some materials are not colorfast. Just be sure you *spot test* a corner or a hidden facing first. I have since used this on pillow slips, and other items, and it worked every time.

Kitchen sponges will last longer if kept clean. Try putting them in with your bath towels in that machine on laundry day. Bet you'll get a surprise.

If you will roll your fitted sheets and fold your top ones, they will be easy to tell apart.

A generous application of paste wax such as one used on hardwood floors, is excellent to apply to the inside of garbage cans (lids too) and wastebaskets. If you use a paper napkin or paper towel the wax will go on much easier and quicker.

## ☙ Dog-Gone Good

This is for those who have pets and use canned dog and cat food that is congealed. I see no need to waste foil and time by covering up a partially used can—or like most of us do, taking out whatever portion we need and setting the can back in the refrigerator where it dries out.

Remove what you need, then turn the can upside down on a saucer or any plastic lid from another product. This sure will keep it from drying out. It won't spill because it's congealed.

When a door or drawer swells and you don't have a carpenter's plane to smooth it down to the proper size— just use a safety razor and it does a beautiful job! It won't cut off much of the wood, but all you usually need is to shave it just a little and it'll fit.

I tried shaving off a hard-to-close screen door with both the double edge and injector types of safety razors, and each works equally well.

## ☙ Roaches Bugging You?

Instead of fighting roaches and never getting rid of them . . . why don't you go looking for them? Let's find where they are laying their eggs. These will be smaller than the eraser on the end of an ordinary pencil and kind of that color too. Wipe them out. They don't play hide-and-seek with me because I take my flashlight every place I think they might be hiding.

You will probably find scads of eggs around the motor of your refrigerator. Look in that tray underneath the motor. Using your flashlight, look above the motor! You will probably find them hanging from the lining in this cozy nook. Use your vacuum cleaner tube to suck all these up and the cobwebs too.

These monsters will lay their eggs on anything they can cling to. Look under all your furniture, especially where anything is rough, such as wood.

Remove the drawers from your kitchen cabinets and take a *long* peek with your flashlight there! Look at the pipes under your sinks in both kitchen and bathroom—especially if you have one of those new built-in vanity cabinets.

Now, if you want to find some more, look under your dining room chairs where the corners are glued with a triangle of wood for reinforcement! These little devils absolutely love glue! Your coffee table and end tables probably have the same thing. Remember, that underneath all the drawers in your dresser and chest this same thing is happening. It's dark—and they love that too.

If you suck them up with your vacuum cleaner, be sure to empty your cleaner after using it. It will be dark and warm in there and they will multiply faster.

Now, if you want to put out bug juice, the time to do it is when you are cleaning these spots. Paint it on while those drawers are opened. (This type is residual for months.)

Remember that your hot water heater in the closet and any place that is warm and dark or has any dampness (such as your dishwasher, or sink) is a good breeding place. Also under your dishwasher, under your stove (just look underneath the burners where all the grease has dropped), your wall oven (after you have removed the entire broiler), under your bathroom sink and the water closet back of the toilet!

Your washing machine is not only warm and dark but damp, too, and that dryer . . . The tops of these two gadgets usually pull open (or the back will). Get your husband to open it up and look at the cobwebs that might be filled with eggs. And each tiny egg "ball" will hatch oodles of roaches—if not destroyed.

Also, look back of your bookshelves! Remove all those books. Remove the dust with your vacuum attachment and apply your bug killer. One of the worst places is your TV set. (Read *caution* labels on hi-voltage before removing the back to clean out the eggs. Better yet, have the repair-man do it for you.) You should see the dust, cobwebs, and roach eggs I've found in testing this hideaway.

Your radios are another good place, and that hi-fi set is their heaven! And look in the back of pianos and organs.

Remember: Darkness, heat, and moisture are potential breeding places for roaches. In one house I went to, these places had all been cleaned. It still had roaches, and guess where I found loads of eggs? Not in the kitchen cabinet, but in the folds and headings of all the draperies!

Draperies (especially if they are heavy draw-drapes) are seldom cleaned. The pleats at the top are usually filled with eggs! Then the little devils even get into the curtain rods! Look inside your curtain rod and see for yourself! Gals, don't waste your time putting bug juice out unless you put it on the right places. Let's kill 'em the easy way.

# Chapter 8

# ℣ On the Job

Having a job means more than working. You may have to travel to get there, eat your lunch away from home, and cope with lots of other little details that are part of the working gal's lot. If, for instance, you work in an office, you'll have a desk that you'll want to keep well-stocked with personal belongings to make your office life more convenient.

There are many wonderful hints to help you gals while on the job.

### ℣ To and Fro

Let's start at the beginning—getting there:

"I am a commuter who used to find waiting for the train a bore—until I learned a good trick involving paperback books. I tear them in halves, thirds and yes, sometimes even fourths! You wonder why?

120

"Well, they can be tucked in a coat pocket or in a purse with no added bulk. Not only does it give me something to do while going back and forth, but at least this is one way to get my reading done.

"I even tore up a Heloise paperback hint book, passed it around to my co-workers and we traded fourths every two days. That made me lots of new friends in the office!"

One paperback book I bought was very thick. I found it was easier to read when torn into parts because lots of us like to turn those little books backward so they are easier to hold onto.

For you folks who commute by car:

If you have a car with leather upholstered seats, put one or two dark colored bath towels, preferably brown, in the car. Keep them rolled up on the floor. Then anytime you park and get out, throw them across the seats.

This keeps the sun off the leather and prevents that "hot seat" problem when you sit in the car later. All you have to do when you come back to the car is remove the bath towels. It will still be warm, I guarantee you, but it won't be blistering and burning like it usually is.

"I carry a heavy white bath towel in my car. When parking in our sunny company parking lot, I fold the towel in half and place it over the steering wheel so it won't get too hot to touch.

"When I remove it from the steering wheel, I place it against the back of the seat to keep my back from touching that hot upholstery."

## 🐾 Carbon Saver

If you're a secretary, I'll bet your boss will love you for this idea: "When answering a letter, turn the paper over and use the back of it for your carbon copy, instead of onion skin paper. Then you have the original letter and the answer all on one sheet of paper. Certainly a saver on filing space, and no stapling or clipping required."

### ❦ *What Price Philosophy?*

I often get letters from working women who say, "Dear Heloise, what is the best advice you can give working women who are just about to smash everything in sight? I am fed up and just about had it. Give me some courage, please . . ."

I want all of those who read this book to take heed (and *that* means pay close attention) to this dissertation, and while you take a few minutes to read this . . . keep in mind that I am *not* a psychiatrist, but have just learned this from all the sweet letters I get from other women who have to work and who pile their troubles up, then pour them out. And I cried when I read some of them . . . I do understand.

I know working gals and wives have hard lives, but it needn't be so. Know what I think is the matter? We work too hard! You think you owe it to your husband and children, but you owe something to yourself, too!

How's about settling for just one hour for yourself once in awhile? It might just make a new woman of you. And don't get a guilt complex about a measly little hour . . . enjoy it. Nobody deserves it more than *you*.

Spend that hour taking a nice hot bath and putting plenty of face cream on your face. While you are in the tub give yourself a foot manicure (I know it's called a pedicure!) So do it while you have a nice, long soak.

### ❦ *Spoil Yourself*

You and your neighbor could agree to baby-sit for each other for a few hours at least once a week. And while your

darlings are gone, utilize that hour literally *spoiling your-self*. If you do nothing but prop your feet up in a chair and stare at the ceiling . . . at *least* do that.

You can keep your friend's childen an hour or so once a week for a few weeks. Let those traded hours pile up, and when you have three or four, take off for a movie. (That's a laugh!)

Don't share these few golden hours with a neighbor or friend. Then it becomes business again. . . . Don't shop. Do something horrible (ha!) like the above. (Here comes your guilt complex again.) There is no one any more important in any home than you. We must preserve ourselves.

Stop and think: If you died tomorrow, what would happen to your family? Believe it . . . the next replacement would not work half as hard as you are doing now. It is not the work that makes you tired. It's the boredom that often goes with the chores. So, change your routine.

Most all of my letters are the same when they come from tired working mothers, and here's the usual routine: Alarm goes off in the morning . . . Yawn . . . Sigh . . . Go to the kitchen in a sleepy daze . . . plug in coffee pot . . . pick up skillet . . . throw bacon in . . . grab eggs . . . butter toast . . . pour coffee, take a sip . . . wake up family . . . yell at kids . . . feed the brood . . . kiss husband good-bye . . . comb kids' hair (yell at 'em again) . . . tell kids good-bye . . . then turn around! Dirty dishes, laundry, unmade beds . . . and *all* to be done before you go to work.

### ❦ *Leave Kitchen*

Just laugh and quit fretting. It happens in every household! For a change, take your coffee into your living room instead of drinking it over the kitchen sink or carrying it around while you are doing your early morning chores and meditate alone for five minutes (nobody deserves it more than you).

At night eat in the dining room (instead of the breakfast room or the kitchen) once in awhile. Then make the family carry their own dishes to the kitchen drainboard.

Try ironing in the living room or on a porch instead of the kitchen! You might be surprised how much faster and more enjoyable ironing might be . . .

Instead of carrying a peanut butter and jelly sandwich to work for your lunch, why not treat yourself to a fancy tuna or chicken salad (it's cheap) . . . maybe even stuffed in a tomato yet! And when you're on your day off at home (That's another laugh. Just what woman *ever* had a day off?), put it on your prettiest plate. (After all, why leave that fancy china for the next generation?) Also, don't eat this in the kitchen. Prop up in bed or on the sofa. It's *yours!*

So enjoy at least one hour a week by spoiling yourself. It's much cheaper than tranquilizers and doctor bills!

### ❦ *For Lasses with Glasses*

"To prevent losing your rings in the office washroom if you absolutely must remove them, slip them over the earpieces of your glasses. They can be easily seen from the corner of your eye and will sure save you from leaving them behind."

"I learned from an optometrist to always wash the nose-piece of my glasses whenever I cleaned the lenses because the oil from a person's skin makes the nosepiece slippery, thereby causing the glasses to slide down."

## ⚘ Be Prepared

Your desk is for more than typing paper, sweetie. Try supplying it with some of these:

"After my deodorant roll-on bottles are empty, I remove the applicator, clean the bottle thoroughly, fill with my favorite cologne, then replace the applicator and top. It's so easy to apply."

Here's a wonderful use for an empty plastic lemon or lime extract dispenser:

"I lifted the little cup (which has the hole in it) from the top of the lemon. I washed the container and filled it with my favorite hand lotion. I always keep one in my desk."

## ⚘ Lunch Time

Bringing your lunch to work can save both money and calories: "I thought you might be interested in the method I use to make *thin* bread for sandwiches to save on calories.

"Freeze the bread, then take out one slice and while it is still frozen, lay it flat on the bread board, and cut through it with a serrated knife.

"If you are making just one sandwich for your own lunch, it is quite simple. If making a great many, be sure to keep the loaf in the freezer and take out only two or three slices at a time, because the minute the bread begins to thaw, it becomes too limp to manage."

A wonderful idea for all of us weight watchers. We'll

still have our sandwich filling "holder" and with half the calories of the regular slices.

Preparing your lunch really doesn't have to be much work.

"When you have to pack lunches every morning, and need some hard-boiled eggs to make egg salad sandwiches: Have soft-boiled eggs for breakfast and hard cook extra ones to use in sandwich spreads.

"The hard-boiled eggs will finish cooking while breakfast is being served. And you won't have an extra pot to wash."

"Ever try using a flat, broad pancake turner to lift sandwiches into a thin plastic or waxed paper sandwich bag?

It's the easiest ever. Keeps the sandwich filling from falling out into the bag. It's so easy, it even makes packing lunches (which isn't my favorite job) seem simple."

Don't think office lunches have to be limited to the same old sandwiches every day: Here's an idea that's especially good for people who work night shift.

"Why not put hot casseroles or spaghetti into a vacuum bottle for a good hot meal? Or if you have one of the large wide-mouthed vacuum bottles, put a couple of small pieces of your cooked chicken into it."

And as a special treat because you're such a good worker:

"I like to have iced tea to drink with my lunch in the summertime. I freeze it in a pint plastic container each day, adding the lemon and sugar before I freeze it.

"By the time I am ready to eat lunch, most of it is melted and I have a big container of iced tea all ready to drink."

"I have an excellent idea for carrying a straw with my lunch. All you have to do is cut an ordinary paper straw in half and lay it in the bag. In that way you can carry it without it sticking out of the bag and bending. It fits just dandy in a milk carton."

And for washing out those plastic cups most of you use for coffee breaks:

"I save the scraps of hand soap and put them into a piece of nylon net about ten inches square. Then I tie two diagonal corners into a knot, reach for the two opposite diagonal corners, and tie them into another knot. I find this a fantastic item for washing plastic coffee cups. It sure cleans that brown film out of them without scratching.

"And never use scouring powder or bleaches on plastic cups. Ruins them. Baking soda is great!"

Don't throw away your oleo cartons. Especially if you pack lunches for work, folks.

Open at one end only and use these to put your sandwiches in after you put it in that plastic bag to keep them from getting mashed—especially if they are tuna fish or egg salad. The best for cake and desserts.

Leftover salads (fruit, potato, chicken, etc.) can be put in baby food jars and kept in your refrigerator a few days.

Plop one in that lunch. Variety is the spice of life. Don't make your lunches dull.

Secretaries and housewives who happen to be using a phone should not put that earring down while they are talking. When they pull it off, they should clip it to the other ear next to the matching one. Sure beats losing an earring.

And when somebody comments (and they are bound to!) about the two earrings on one ear, it will be a good opportunity to pass the hint along and save others from losing theirs, too.

Rinse out a plastic-coated milk carton, pour your left-over, cool coffee into this and set the carton inside your freezer.

Each day you can remove the carton and add more cool coffee until it is full. When full and solidly frozen, turn the carton on its side and take your ice pick and jab, jab, jab away. Keep turning the carton over and punch all sides full of holes.

This makes the most wonderful crushed coffee-ice you have ever seen. The top of the carton may be opened and the ice pours directly into a glass or thermos.

This is great for iced coffee, and when put into sweet milk, it gives the milk a slight coffee taste.

Or it may just be poured into a little bowl and eaten as is. Those who are ice chewers will especially like this. Quite an uplift.

Save your pickled beet juice and put some cottage cheese in it. Drain off the white fluid from the cottage cheese before you put it in the beet juice. You'll end up with pink pickled cottage cheese and it is really terrific!

# Chapter 9

# ✌ *Gloop & Glop*

These are quickie tidbits that just seem to fit in any home and we know you'll just love them. They're real time savers:

Old yellowed newspaper clippings can be bleached white again by soaking them in a weak solution of household bleach and water. Rinse well and slap it on your refrigerator door to dry. Be like new again.

Know those automatic elevators with the magic-eye push buttons? The ones you just touch with your finger, the light comes on and elevator goes? If you ever have both arms loaded with groceries or bundles don't waste your time putting your packages down.

Just touch the button with your nose and up she goes . . . it gives the same end result.

For all those dolls who forget to turn off the lights when parking a car . . . if you keep a snap-on clothespin on your sun visor it will not only help hold those letters and notes that must be mailed but when you turn the lights on reach for that clothespin and snap it on your ignition key.

When you reach your destination and turn off the motor, the clothespin on the key will remind all absentminded professors and overworked homemakers to turn those blinkers off. Sure saves money for repairing run-down batteries.

Now . . . if we could find a way to keep from running down our own bodies and minds, wouldn't that just be something?

If you live upstairs or have a basement, *don't* make the mistake of trying to carry each sack, bag, and bundle up all the steps at one time then come back down for the next one. You can "walk" your packages too! Save *your* energy by using the following method:

Save all the items to be carried on a lower step and move them up two or three steps at a time, walk up, move them up a few more steps again . . . and so on.

The same method can be used going down too, and only one trip is necessary.

Before closing up any summer cabin for the winter, turn all the drawers (bedroom, bath, and kitchen) upside down. The rodents and mice cannot make nests in them. Residual roach killer on the bottom of each drawer, too, is a grand idea. Mothballs are also a must too. And do leave that refrigerator door *open*—wide open.

If you drill small holes in the bottom of your barbecue

grill, you can put water on the coals as soon as the meat has finished cooking and save them for next time.

The water will drain out. Also, if you leave it outside (and just who doesn't) when it rains, this will prevent a collection of water in the bottom and thus prevent rusting. Saves more dimes and dollars!

Here's one of the greatest ideas that has come along since we landed man on the moon:

On the sun visor in your car *and* in your billfold, *always* put the name of your parents and one of your neighbors and their phone numbers in case of accident. Reason? If we are out "cold," the first thing that any policeman or hospital does is to look for someone to notify. Your entire family might just be with you when that accident happens. Then what?

Usually a neighbor knows more about you than you think. She can always find some kinfolks to help. The name of your personal physician should *also* be included—along with your next of kin.

Pick up a pen right now and jot this information down and stick it in your purse. Next time you are in your car you can tape or clip it to that sun visor. May save confusion and heartache in an emergency.

And for the gals who wash their own cars—that kitchen string mop is good for something besides the floor. Try washing the car with it.

Especially good for shorties, and since it's so much bigger than a rag or sponge, it covers more space. Quicker—and no water running down your arms when you try to wash the top and hood.

Shake a thermometer down while it's still in the case. Easier to hold and should you drop it, it won't break.

Do you know the number of steps in any flight of stairs in your home? You certainly *should!*

If you are carrying something bulky that prevents your seeing the steps, or you're in a hurry . . . just count them as you go down and you will know when you have reached the bottom. Real good for those whose sight is impaired.

Battles are fought and many are lost, but I don't think I ever heard of many women permanently winning the battle of the toilet bowl ring. . . . Have you? I think I found the cause of 90 percent of our troubles. I have made tests in hard water areas, and most of this kind of water leaves rings of discolorations and stains. These are definitely caused by minerals in the water—which none of us can do too much about.

But . . . we can take the top of the tank off and see what's down inside. I nearly dropped dead when I saw what was in two of them. One tank bottom was covered with hard mud and tiny bits of built-up minerals. The other was loaded with orange rust in the bottom and the sides were completely coated with it.

This is what caused that discolored bowl each week. If the bottom of the tank is covered with minerals and rust, it stands to reason that some of it is bound to end up in the bowl. So let's go clean out those water tanks.

Remove as much of the hard residual as possible. Then use an old sponge and try to pick up what's left. I did and so can you.

Wipe all the discoloration off the insides. Gals, that water is going to be so muddy looking that you will wonder where the bottom went! Now start flushing. Not once but lots of times. Each time wipe the inside with the sponge again until all the discoloration comes off. This may also be cleaned with scouring powder. Then just flush again until it's spanking clean.

I cross my heart that if you get this job done, that bowl won't get stained so quickly.

Use a sandwich-size plastic bag over your hand when scouring pans with a soap pad. When you're finished, just pull the pad into the bag kind of wrong side out as your hand slips out. You can then wrap the scrubber to store for another time, or throw it away.

Saves hands and no more wet, rusty pads under the sink!

If you put a soap-filled steel wool pad in a peanut butter jar, fill it with hot water, cap it, then shake a bit and leave it overnight, you will find the most wonderful cleaning goop imaginable. It lasts for weeks this way, and can be used over and over.

Each time you use the pad, rinse it out and replace under the mixture. Never rusts. Gee, I love to save pennies, don't you?

### ❦ Easy Dishwashing

Now . . . for those who don't have dishwashers, take heed and mark my word for it. There *is* an easy way to do dishes and save time without putting your hands in hot water and suds.

First thing you do is plug up your sink and pour some detergent in it. (Lots of folks like to rinse and stack them first.) Then turn on your hot water faucet and let 'er fill up with nice suds. (Use *no* cold water.)

Put your silver in the bottom, then scrape plates (used paper napkins are great for this). Scrape all the "leavings" into a newspaper, roll it up and toss into the pail. Then put your glasses on top of the dishes and forget them. Literally, I mean.

Only when that water gets *cold,* and *only* then . . . reach into that sink and pull out that plug and let all the water drain away. Turn on your hot water faucet and, using a sponge or brush, gently rinse all your dishes and put in your drainer.

While your dishes have been washing themselves *you,* my dears, can be straightening up your little home in other ways. Or doing more important things such as resting a bit! At least your kitchen will have that clean look as "they" are under water. Your cabinets, the table, and drainboard are straightened.

Many working gals just leave them under plain warm water when they leave for work (especially if they are late) and do this when they get home: pour straight liquid detergent on a wet sponge (saves detergent), wipe each article with the suds it makes and rinse. Voilà!

Under any circumstances . . . *don't* ever put your hands in hot water when you don't have to.

All you gals who work so hard to save those pennies (that make dimes, and dimes make dollars) learn to save on paper towels too. Once they have been used to dry your hands on, or wipe up the water from your drainboard . . . are you aware that they can be reused again? True!

They are great for wiping out food from dishes and those pots and pans before plunking dishes in your dishwater. Just try using them in place of a sponge or dishcloth. They have just enough roughage that they do a great scouring job.

And just wait until you clean your sink with that scouring powder. That wet secondhand towel is absolutely perfect, folks. No more wet dishcloths hanging up to dry. So sanitary too.

And one adorable friend said that if you have a problem of draining cutlery while washing dishes, you know that a glass accumulates water in the bottom, a "store-bought" holder often topples over, and cutlery put in the rack is a nuisance to gather.

She discovered that an ordinary clay flower pot with the small drainage hole in the bottom works very well. It's heavy enough to stay upright, the water can flow out, and it's attractive on the drainboard.

Use a plastic lace place mat in the bottom of your kitchen sink. It prevents marks from pots and pans and catches little articles that might go down the drain.

Because it's plastic, it doesn't stick like rubber. It can be easily washed and bleached and it also looks nice in the sink.

If you have an upright vacuum cleaner with the beater brushes on the bottom and it doesn't seem to be cleaning lately, why not try this? Turn the vacuum over on its side and just look at that beater. You're going to find it's probably tied and gagged—brushes and all—with hair, strings, and such . . .

Remove the beater. Usually all you have to do is lift a little lever that holds it in and slide the roller out of the belt and bracket. Spread a sheet of newspaper on the floor and lay the roller on it. Then either get your scissors or a sharp knife. Now, literally "whack" with the knife or cut with your scissors through all of those hairs and thread. These must be cut between each row of brushes on the roller. Some have two, some have three or four rows.

*Gloop & Glop*    135

Don't try to remove it any other way. Here's why: If you cut only one side and try to pull them loose, it's going to take too much of your time. Besides, every time you pull on a long thread, it gets embedded deeper in the brushes. If you have cut these up like I have told you, all you have to do is to pull them loose from the brushes. Easy as pie. Then clean the brushes with a stiff brush.

And while you are at it, remove that bag and clean it out too. You'll be surprised how much cleaner your carpets will get next time you use that vacuum. It seems like most women think to empty the bag but never look at the brushes to see what has accumulated on them.

This might save you a repair bill.

Many people complain that when they raise their windows the breeze doesn't come in. If that's your problem, too, take a close look at your screens. When there's an accumulation of dust on them, the breeze cannot get through —especially in the summertime when you need them the most.

Besides, a screen that has dust sticking on it dirties up your windows each time the wind blows or it rains.

Let's talk about woodwork: Annoying subject, but it is something we all have and will have the rest of our life. So let's figure out a way to clean it without ruining it.

Be *very* careful what you wash painted woodwork with. Lots of products will get it clean, but might remove some of your expensive paint.

Here's how to test the cleaner you are using on your painted walls: Take a dark-colored washcloth (if your paint is white or light) and use your present cleaner (according to directions) to clean a small area of your woodwork.

Before rinsing the cloth, *look* at it to see if there is any white paint on it! Dirt, soil, fingerprints, and grime just *ain't* white. If your cloth has light stains on it you are removing some of your paint.

If this happens, change your brand of woodwork cleaner quick. Keep changing and testing until you find a product that passes this test. Many people write to me and say, "My paint was no good, it washes off." After checking it out, we have learned it usually was the cleaner after all.

Paint jobs are expensive, so take care of them. That money saved can be used for other things.

If you buy onions or potatoes in a red or yellow plastic sack, do save the sack. I used them the same way I use nylon net for dishcloths. Just put your dishcloth inside and scrub away. Oh, how nice for pots and pans!

Also, I have covered many worn and torn sponges with plastic onion and vegetable bags, and they give a most satisfactory result.

I save, wash, fold, and store all empty milk and oleo cartons and use them to start the fire in our fireplace. These cartons can also be used for an outdoor fireplace or a campfire. The wax on the cartons makes the cardboard burn far faster, and in no time you have a nice fire going.

Don't bother to hand wash an electric blender when it can wash itself in no time.

One owner says: "Do you know that many of us won't use our blenders because they are so hard to clean? I was just as foolish as the rest of the women at a cooking school until our instructor gave us this simple method which is real quick and easy.

"After using, rinse the blender with clear water. Then half fill with warm water and put in three or four drops of liquid detergent. Put on the cover and be sure to hold it down firmly with the palm of your hand while you turn the switch to *low*.

"Let this run for a moment or so. Empty and rinse with clear water. Just don't put in too much detergent or run the blender on high. You will have excessive suds."

"For the people who hang out washing . . . If you'll take a card table, sprinkling bottle, and plastic bag to your

clothesline, you can sprinkle your clothes, sort, and fold them as you take them down.

"The warm sun on your sprinkled clothes when folded does wonders for your ironing. Saves many steps, too!"

Use a small, new powder puff for greasing pots and pans. Keep it in the shortening can ready for use anytime.

I've learned something that has saved me a lot of work. After cleaning the top of my refrigerator, I covered it with clear plastic wrap. Since it is transparent, you can hardly tell it is there.

When the wrap becomes dusty or soiled, just peel it off and replace it with fresh wrap. This eliminates scrubbing the top of the refrigerator, and the finish stays like new.

"I have a hint on laundering synthetic draperies. The directions that came with mine said not to use soap, as the fiber is actually glass and the dirt is only encasing the thread.

"The first time, I washed mine without soap, and they had big yellow stains bleeding from the top. As the drapes are white, the stain really showed. Next time, I used a mild detergent and soaked them for a few minutes before hand washing. Then I used a mild vinegar rinse, hung them *upside down* on the line and they are beautiful.

"I discovered that though the drapes themselves are made of glass, the heading inside is made of porous fiber which holds dirt and soil. Dirt bleeding out of the heading had *caused* the stains before!"

The pleater tape, facing, or lining along the top of any draperies collects what we call carbon. This is a yellow stain and is caused by everyday fumes in our homes from cooking, smoking, heating systems, etc.

If you doubt this, some day put a few drops of ammonia on your kitchen window before you wash it, and when it runs down watch how yellow the run turns. That's carbon, too!

"Have you ever accidentally put a plastic wrapper (like bread comes in) on *hot* chrome, such as a toaster or a waffle iron? Of course, the plastic melts and it is very difficult to take off without scratching the surface of the chrome!

"One day I tried fingernail polish remover, and presto! The plastic came off slick as a whistle!"

"After removing a piece of plastic wrap from anything, I just stick it on the refrigerator door. It will cling there itself until I am ready to use it again."

Too often our dishwater is cold before the worst items —pots and pans—have been washed.

If water is heated on the stove in one of those yet-to-be scrubbed pans while the first dishes and silver are being washed, the extra hot water is readily available to pour in your dishwater when you reach those last hard-to-clean pieces.

To remove candle drippings or wax from table tops, just use your hair dryer and turn it on warm until the wax softens a bit.

Pick up the big chunks and then use a facial tissue or paper napkin and rub the rest away. It works like magic and leaves no scars.

Ever try to remove candle wax from your candlesticks (silver or otherwise), only to have it turn into a sticky mess?

Just pop them into the freezer for a couple of hours until the wax is frozen and you can remove those drippings with a flick of your fingernail!

Cast iron skillets are kept in good condition with the following treatment:

Season (before use) by greasing with shortening that contains *no* salt.

Never use detergent on them and as little steel wool as possible. Just scalding hot water and a kitchen brush.

Keep skillets stored in your oven. Place them there immediately after the oven has been in use, and the dry heat keeps them from rusting.

Some people put them back over the burner after washing until they get slightly hot and then rub it with crumpled up waxed paper. This puts a coating on them that will also prevent rust.

And the American Walnut Manufacturers wrote:

"The finest walnut furniture can be washed with soap and water if the water used is not excessive.

"Once or twice a year a mild soap and water solution can be used, with a cloth well wrung out and rubbed over the surface. Rinse off soap.

"The furniture should then be rubbed dry with a fresh cloth. The cleaning removes most smears and stickiness. Fresh waxing can follow. This is most beneficial in restoring the luster of antique furniture.

"Here is a cleaning formula that also works: Put one teaspoon of olive oil and one teaspoon of turpentine in a quart of warm water. Swish a cloth in this mixture. Press out excess moisture from the cloth and rub down the furniture. Follow by *drying* with another cloth. Fresh wax can be applied later.

"In all cases, overwaxing of fine walnut furniture should be avoided. Waxing once or twice a year is often enough."

### ❦ Tile Film?

I think the *"Tile Council of America"* has answered our problem and I think they are the greatest when they mention one of my favorite words: "Kerosene." Take heed to the following advice:

"Being in the tile business, we thought your readers might be interested in these few tips on the care of ceramic tile.

"Glazed ceramic tile on walls seldom requires special cleaning except to remove a film which may result from the splashing of soapy water, or caused by the combination of soap and minerals in 'hard' water.

"In such cases, the best cleanser is a soapless detergent, although a scouring powder can be used also.

"If cleaning has been neglected to the extent that there is a heavy accumulation of dirty film, it may be necessary to use a stiff bristle brush. Do not expect that a single application of detergent will remove a stubborn coating of grime. Be sure to rinse the tile thoroughly and wipe dry with an old turkish towel. This will add sparkle to the tile wall.

"As for heel marks and smudges that remain after a simple mopping, they may be removed by scrubbing with an abrasive type cleaner, an application of kerosene, or by rubbing with a soft rubber pencil eraser."

Many, many people have written in and told me different ways to dry sweaters. If you have a dryer, naturally the best thing is to lay it on top and stretch it to size and let it dry there. Other people dry them on screens, and so on.

Well, you know those aluminum folding chairs that have woven plastic in the bottom and back? This is the greatest for drying sweaters! The reason is that the air comes up from the bottom . . . it's webbed, you know.

If you have an old chair, I do suggest to put a bath towel over it first. These chairs accumulate soil. That's why our clothes sometimes get dirty when we're sitting on them in white shorts or slacks. These chairs need to be washed from time to time.

So the next time you're watering your garden, wash down those chairs, too. They dry quickly and the aluminum and plastic are not harmed by water.

During the summer, our bathing suits are left hither and thither. *Don't* leave chlorine or salt water in the bathing suit. They not only deteriorate the fabric but fade the color.

Any time you come back from swimming in salt water,

chlorinated water, or any type of swimming pool (whether private or community), wash your bathing suit . . . not in just plain water, but with a good detergent . . . and rinse it well. This prevents fading and rotting.

*Never* sit, lie, or stretch out on concrete (that's cement) in any type of elasticized bathing suit. Always put a bath towel down *first*. This prevents cutting of the fibers in the suit. Save any way you can, especially when bathing suits are so expensive nowadays.

And if your slipcovers look as if they are on their last lap . . . try another reader's hint: "Here is a suggestion that may help those ladies who want to give their living rooms a pickup but haven't the money for new slipcovers.

"The cover on our sofa was in pretty bad shape, and I couldn't replace it at that time. The arms and both sides of the seat cushions were worn and faded (as they get the most wear), but the material on the back of the sofa was in perfect condition.

"I used the material on the back of the sofa to replace the tops of the worn cushions. And there was still enough cloth left to put a strip on top of each arm between the piping. I replaced the material I had used from the back with some sheeting so the cover would retain its shape.

"The result was a nice, fresh looking sofa cover that even the children thought was new, and there was no strain at all on our budget."

### ❦ Baking Spills
What price casseroles? But . . . oh, when they drip on that oven!

No matter how hard we try to keep our oven clean when we bake in it, once in awhile we'll fill the baking utensil too full and that casserole or pie just boils over. Quite by accident I learned something real tricky last week.

Know those old throw-away frozen dinner pans and pie pans we all save? What are they good for? Ah-ha . . . see where the multitude of drips are coming from, and slide one of these pans under that very spot on the shelf below.

I have now learned that when I bake something that might drip or overflow, I can take two of these wonderful pans and put them on the floor of my oven just in case there are drips. These can be used over and over again.

It came to my attention recently that some of you aren't taking full advantage of your refrigerators. If you have one, it probably has a large shallow drip tray beneath the ice freezer compartment. Is yours empty?

It shouldn't be. Do you realize that you can dump four or more ice cube trays into this one large drip pan and always have cubes at hand when you want them? They won't melt.

Just think how many times a day children run in for a cool drink or plain old ice to crunch. How nice if they can simply slide out that tray, grab a chunk, and be on their way!

Constant refilling of ice cube trays and dripping water across the floor would be cut to a minimum. And no more running out of ice just before you're ready to serve iced drinks.

What's more, every time that freezing unit door is opened the hot air rushes inside and the ice will build up quickly to the point where you'll have to defrost more often . . . and who likes that job?

This is a real time-saver—the perfect storage spot for those extra ice cubes. Put it to use!

## 🌱 *Shower Curtain Mildew?*

And for those of you who want to prevent mildew along the bottom of your shower curtain . . .

Many people write that they take a pair of pinking scissors and cut that hem off where the water collects. This allows all of the water to drip off instead of just sitting there. If you don't have pinking scissors, just use your regular snips.

And when you wash that shower curtain, be *sure* to put it in with your bath towels. The roughness of the terry cloth rubs against the slickness of the curtain in your washing machine, making for a real neat job.

Many of you write:

"We have just moved, and our new home has a recreation room in the basement. Mildew is forming on the walls and rubber tile floor. How can we get rid of it and what will prevent it from reappearing?"

Following is what the *U.S. Department of Agriculture* has to say about it:

"Mildew thrives in hot, humid weather. High moisture causes the mold spores, which are always present in the air, to settle and grow on shoes, clothing, furniture, and books.

"The best protection against mildew is, of course, in its prevention. And to prevent mildew, you must remove its cause—the dampness. Because cool air holds less moisture than warm air, air conditioners are helpful. Dehumidifiers are useful where moisture is a problem.

"You can also fight off dampness by heating the house for a short time. Then open the doors and windows to let the moist air out. An exhaust fan will help force it out.

"To dry the air in closets and other small areas, keep a

small electric light burning in the top of the closet. The heat will be enough to prevent mildew if the space is not too large.

"A safe way to keep a closet dry is with silica gel or activated alumina. These chemicals will absorb the moisture in the air. Hang them in a cloth bag from the closet rod, or put them on a shelf. The chemicals can be used over and over. (You simply dry them in a vented oven at 300 degrees for several hours.)

And for those who just can't afford hot oil treatments on their tresses . . . listen to this humdinger: "You absolutely won't believe it until you try it, but this is the most fabulous thing that has ever happened to my budget . . . and my hair.

"My beauty operator knew I couldn't possibly afford professional treatments for my dry, dull, lifeless, and bleached hair. So she suggested that I buy a pint of real mayonnaise to use on my hair at home.

"She told me to take a handful of it and rub into my scalp, and then comb it through my hair and leave it at least thirty minutes before every home shampoo. (Wrap an old towel around your head because eventually the mayonnaise begins to run or drip!)

"It's amazing! Life began to come back into my dry, brittle hair after only a few treatments. Maybe others who can't afford expensive treatments can save this way, too."

Well, now, don't laugh at this idea because by golly, it actually works. At first I couldn't believe it, but then I got to thinking: There are hot oil shampoos, plain oil shampoos, and egg shampoos. And both eggs and oil are in mayonnaise! So, I called some cosmetologists.

They all agreed that it works. When they find a person

who needs hair conditioners, they recommend this treatment when the customer can't afford other treatments!

They also said that it couldn't hurt any head of hair that they knew of unless someone was *allergic* to mayonnaise or its condiments. (You can test this by rubbing some on the inside of the arm along the elbow, and leaving it for an hour.)

Since my hair is not dyed, bleached, or dry, and hadn't been teased so that it was broken . . . I couldn't try it on me. But I told nine girl friends about it, and every one of them thought it was a great idea because it was inexpensive, and mayonnaise was usually in the home and handy. Also, it was easy to remove with a shampoo and their hair was really reconditioned.

Some used three heaping tablespoonsful (according to the thickness and texture of their hair) and two (who had long, thick, hair) used half a pint!

So try it if you wish. I don't guarantee anything, but you really have nothing to lose except a few spoonsful of mayonnaise.

# Chapter 10

# ❧ Hello, Tootsie!

When we're home, most of us settle into a comfortable pair of loafers or even go barefoot—as I do. No stockings to buy, wash, or run! And no stiff high heeled shoes to pinch and give us blisters!

But for most working gals, every day means real shoes and stockings. This is probably one of the greatest expenses —and greatest problems—we girls have.

But it doesn't have to be! And to do your job well, it shouldn't be. After all, if those tootsies are killing you, you just can't be as cheerful and efficient as you have to. I've gotten letters from saleswomen, teachers, nurses—and these jobs sure involve plenty of standing—asking me if there's anything they can do to make being on their feet all day less painful. Well there *is*. And all of us—whether we stand in front of a stove or sink, or behind a lingerie counter—should take care of our feet.

## ✿ Goody, New Shoes

For openers, there's much you can do right at the start, when you buy your shoes. I've gotten this information right from the horse's mouth (well, actually, from the *American Podiatry Association* in Washington, D.C. and Mr. Francis A. Kalbacher):

"Don't buy shoes in the morning because your feet *can* stretch as much as half a size by the afternoon.

"A prime consideration is to fit the shoes to the feet, *not* the feet to the shoes.

"Always stand up when your feet are being measured and when you try on new shoes, for feet usually lengthen out when they are supporting your body weight. Do not count on breaking shoes in when the feet have expanded from previous hours of standing or walking. The difference can be one-half a shoe size!

"Shoes should be allowed to 'rest' after a day's wear. This rest period allows the shoes to dry out.

"People should not try to break in shoes by wearing them out of the store.

"In the first place, shoes that require much breaking in are probably a wrong fit.

"In the second place, once shoes are worn outdoors and become scuffed there is little likelihood the shoe salesman will permit you to return them.

"Covering a pair of new shoes with an old pair of socks will protect them from scuffs as you initially wear them for short periods around the house.

"New shoes should be worn for short periods of time rather than all day.

"It is wrong to blame all foot troubles on shoes. Shoes can be one of the aggravating causes and then it is usually the fit, not the shoe itself. Customers are as guilty for poor fit as are shoe salesmen.

"Changing two or three different pairs of shoes a day is a good habit.

"Inexpensive shoes are not necessarily harmful to good foot health. More important, it is the fit that counts. Even expensive shoes, if improperly fitted, will aggravate foot conditions."

### 🐾 Big Foot Forward

Is one shoe too tight? Here's what one gal learned from her shoe salesman.

"One foot is often slightly larger than the other, so it's wise to buy your shoes to fit the larger foot. Then, buy a pair of innersoles and insert one in the shoe for the smaller foot."

### Blister Blues?

If there's one thing worse than going to work with tight shoes, it's going with blisters, corns, or calluses! Several of you gals have had some super ideas on solving this problem:

How many people get what I call "shoe-bite" from new shoes? "To eliminate blisters from forming on my feet, I take a new, dry bar of baby soap and rub soap on the inside of my shoes before I ever wear them.

"There will be a collection of soap chips, which I then rub into the leather *inside* the shoe with my fingertips. I rub the sides, upper part where the toes touch, and the innersole where the foot rests.

"I do this with every new pair of shoes that I get (including slippers), and my troubles are over!"

"I let both feet soak until the water gets cool (and hope the phone doesn't ring in the meantime), then rub briskly with the heavy towel. It makes a new person out of me!"

"My feet are much more comfortable when I put facial tissues in my shoes when wearing stockings." (This is a great idea even when you do not wear stockings.)

Many women complain that when wearing nylon stockings their feet perspire. So after putting on your stockings, fold a facial tissue to fit the bottom of your foot, leaving just a bit to tuck back up over your shoes. Then put your foot in your shoe.

You will be surprised to see how damp that tissue is at the end of the day! And when worn *over* stockings, it won't stick to your foot.

### Tired Dogs

While I go barefoot most of the time and don't have too much foot trouble, I've found the best thing for tired feet is to make some good suds in a bucket of warm water, throw a bath towel on the floor in front of my favorite chair, and plop those feet in the warm water while I'm watching TV or reading the newspaper. Wow!

You know those loafers that we buy? Well, eventually we all love to wear them without socks. That's when they get soiled inside. Especially if they are not lined with leather or washable materials.

So I buy mine a half-size larger than usual and at the same time buy innersoles to put inside them. This way they hug my tootsies, yet all I have to do is remove the innersoles and wash them!

So next time when you buy a pair of loafers or have an old pair that have stretched, why not put innersoles in them?

### Mirror Bright

If you've ever seen a military parade, you must have noticed how the marchers' shoes and boots shine like mirrors. You know how they do it? They use paste wax and buff the shoes with a brush. Then they use a cloth. Some use nylon stockings. This gives a real good shine.

Then they reapply more wax with a soft cloth, not a brush this time. The shoes are buffed again with a soft cloth after they flick a little cold water on the toes.

Others actually spit on their shoes and buff again with the soft cloth. This is where the expression "spit and polish" came from. Ask any paratrooper or parade marcher. He'll tell you.

You can use the same method and your shoes will really knock them out at the office. And your hubby and little ones will really appreciate this kind of shine too!

Here's another fine hint on how to keep your shoes in top condition for work or play:

"We have often seen men dust off the toes of their shoes on the back of their pants leg.

"Our shoeshine parlor always has strips of men's wool pants cut up to buff these shoes. The wool really makes them shine. So why not cut up some old pieces of wool to shine your shoes?"

And for those people who wear rubber slip-on sandals, are you aware that they can be washed in the washing machine along with bath towels? Sure gets them clean.

Here's another cute trick: "I hang my nylon hose by both top and toe on the line, so that the wind can't toss them on the clothespins."

And from a real honey pie: "If you hate the mess of untangling your nylons after washing several pair at a time, do this: When you are ready to launder them, pick up one stocking from your collection and draw it up full-length over your arm like a glove. Pull another one on over that, then another and another until you have them all on your arm.

"Then slip them off your arm as one piece, wash as one, and hang as one. They take the space of only one on your drying rack. They will dry beautifully and come apart easily."

Just think of the snags this idea is going to save! Put an old stocking on the outside.

If you're ever in a hurry for a clean pair of hose, you can dry them quickly in your dryer cap. Just turn it on medium and they'll be dry in no time.

### ❦ Bags and Sags
Here's a really great idea: "If your nylon stockings seem to bag or sag on your legs, just wet your hands in warm water and starting from the ankles, rub your damp hands *up* your leg. This sure makes them fit better."

### Hosiery Chic
It's fun to try all the colored and patterned stockings that are so popular now. There's no reason why you can't have the most "with it" legs in your office!

"When wearing fishnet hose, slip on a pair of footlets before putting on the hose. It's not only more comfortable, but saves wearing holes in the fishnet."

Here's what I call a beautiful idea:
"If you wear support stockings, but want a darker shade,

just wear a darker shade of sheer hose over them. No one will know the difference.

"This can be done with sheer, lighter shades of stockings, too."

If you love to wear bright-colored stockings, like green and red, or purple, you'll appreciate something I just learned. It's a trick based on a tried-and-true method.

Buy a package of all-purpose dye. Take your *oldest* unmated stockings and tint them to wear with those new dresses.

I did not even boil my stockings. I put my teakettle on the stove and brought the water to a boil, poured the package of dye into a stainless steel pan, held my teakettle high and slowly poured the boiling water over the dye, then stirred it well with a spoon.

You'll be amazed what pretty colors of pink, red, and blue you can get. Why buy them when you have unmated stockings anyway? Or "more better yet," tint those light-colored ones which look like they're faded. So, gals, let's get with it!

"For a quick touch-up on white suede shoes try regular white chalk."

I've found a real neat way to keep white tennis shoes cleaned: "After washing and drying the shoes, I polish them with white polish, and when the polish is dry, I spray the shoes with spray starch. I can wear them a lot longer without washing them because the dirt brushes right off."

When I wash out stockings and small articles in the sink, I always use one of our flexible plastic glasses as a plunger to help remove the soil. Just fill up the basin with hot sudsy water and put the garments in. Then squash up and down with that plastic glass.

I found it did a great job when the *open* end of the glass was turned *down*. And you won't boil your hands!

# Chapter 11

# *Some Like It Cold*

And cold is what usually goes into a lunchbox—husband's, children's, and especially the working gal's. Cold is easy and economical, and when prepared and served imaginatively, delicious and healthful too. Cold goes on picnics. And also to church suppers and buffet lunches. Candy

and those rich desserts we all love are cold, too. So be it sandwich, salad, or what-have-you, cold food can be a boon to the busy woman.

Now here's a helpful shortcut:

"When I cut sandwiches, I don't make a complete cut through the bottom slice of bread. This way they are easier to slip into the sandwich bags and can easily be pulled apart when they're to be eaten."

You sandwich eaters heed this one:

"For those who often eat sandwiches, here's a little trick I learned that saves me time and keeps the bread fresh.

"When I bring a loaf home from the store, I put two slices in little plastic sandwich bags and fold them over or staple them. Then I put all the bags in the crisper of my refrigerator.

"When I need bread for a sandwich, I remove one envelope and the rest is undisturbed."

The bread manufacturers tell me that frozen bread does not age. They also say it can be kept frozen indefinitely if held airtight with plastic. So if you have room in the freezing compartment of your refrigerator, keep your bread in there. It's a good idea for those who live alone, or who are on special diets and must not eat too much bread, to do only a half loaf this way and put the remaining half in your freezer.

Your little individual plastic sandwich sacks may be used over and over again and need *not* be wasted.

Attractive looking sandwiches are always welcome:

"Did you know that a serrated steak knife will make the prettiest shell design when spreading cream cheese, or any spread, on crackers and dainty sandwiches? Really makes them look festive!"

(Have you ever tried using that serrated blade to spread cake icing? Try that sometime. Real perky!)

*Some Like It Cold*    157

Here's another tip for those who make tiny or fancy sandwiches. If you find you can't cut the crust off without tearing or smashing the bread, just try using an electric knife! It is absolutely lush and easy. Never tears at all.

### ❦ Salad Days

Two sure-fire tricks from the pros:

"As a restaurant owner, I believe that many women would like to know what sometimes causes lettuce salads to wilt. It's salt! If one wants to serve a salad as crisp as those in restaurants, never put the salt on until just before serving it.

"Restaurateurs never salt their lettuce salads when placing them on the serving table. The salt is always added immediately before the salad is served to each individual. Consequently, they do not wilt or become tough."

(You know, gals, this is true! And don't put the dressing on until immediately before the salad is served. This is why dressings are usually served on the side.)

"I am a salad girl in one of a famous chain of restaurants, and I would like your readers to know how we core lettuce for our lovely salads.

"First, soak it in cold salt water to get any soil out of the lettuce.

"Put the lettuce on a wooden board with the stem end up. Hit the core of the lettuce with your fist two or three times.

"Twist out the core with your fingers.

"Then hold the lettuce under the water faucet, letting the cool water flow into this hole you have made by removing the core portion.

"The head of lettuce will separate beautifully and be clean!"

Salads are great for picnics:

"For those who go on picnics and like to keep salads cool: I put my salad in the bottom of a double boiler, ice cubes in the top part, and plop on the lid. Keeps the salad really cool and tasty."

And when you get to the picnic and need a few cubes of ice for that soft drink, you can reach right in the top of the boiler and pick 'em out!"

And for picnics, there's nothing like a good potato salad. I've learned something real tricky. If you're fixing potato salad in the morning (and I think this is the best time to make it), boil your eggs and potatoes while you are washing dishes.

After making the salad, we usually cover it with a piece of plastic and put it in the refrigerator. You sometimes find that moisture forms on the inside of the plastic and drips down onto the salad.

Here's what to do! Put a paper towel or napkin over the top of the contents of the bowl first, and *then* put the plastic over it. The napkin will absorb the moisture that accumulates on the plastic.

Instead of having a water-logged salad, you will have a delicious one, just as you prepared it!

We all love egg salad, and here's a mussless, fussless way to prepare it:

"When I make egg salad, I use my egg slicer to slice the eggs. I slice the egg one way, and holding it together I pick it up, turn it around and slice it in the opposite direction.

"I have nice cubes of egg just right for mixing and no messy grater to wash."

*Some Like It Cold*    159

The following is one of the most delicious salads I've ever tasted: "I'm in the restaurant business and have a recipe that's ever so good.

"We often use this recipe in sandwiches and stuffed tomatoes. Or just place it on a big leaf of lettuce and top it with a spoonful of salad dressing, a dash of paprika, and a green stuffed olive. This is one of the best sellers in our restaurant. Here's how it's made:

"Use one can of light, grated tuna. We use grated because it costs less. Mash or squeeze all of the oil out, if you cannot find tuna packed in brine.

"Then put it in a mixing bowl. Grate one small apple on the smallest part of your grater into the tuna and add the juice of one-half lemon.

"Now take any leftover meats that you have in your refrigerator such as lean pieces of ham, pork, beef, or chicken (whether it's fried, boiled, or baked, use it), and grind it in your meat grinder. Then add to the mixture. While your meat grinder is out, also grind a few sweet pickles into the mixture.

"It doesn't really make any difference how much other meat you add to this so long as you start with *one* can of tuna fish. Add just enough salad dressing to the mixture to make it the consistency that you prefer. Chill thoroughly before serving.

"Any one, two, or even three different kinds of meat can be ground up into this mixture at the same time. To vary it, some days we use ham, the next day we use pork, and maybe turkey the following day."

### ❦ *Always Handy*

If you have a blender, here's a dandy suggestion.

Remove the skin from a boiled chicken which has been left in the refrigerator at least twenty-four hours. Then get

right down to the meat itself—back, neck, thigh, wings—
and pull it from the bones.

Now put this meat in your blender (*don't* put in the
skin) and *do not add any water or liquid whatsoever!*

Turn the blender on real quick and then turn it off.
While it's off, push the chicken down off the sides of the
blender so the blades can reach it again. Do this three or
four times. You'll have the most beautiful chopped chicken
you've ever seen in your life. (If you don't have a blender,
use your meat grinder.)

Drop it in a plastic bag, twist the top, place a rubber
band around it (or store in a plastic jar), and stack it in
your freezing compartment or deep freezer.

So help me, you can dip out one tablespoon, pour out
half a bag or just as much as you want to use with egg
noodles, in salads, casseroles, or baby's first solid food. Real
great, too, for hors d'oeuvres (try mixing it with sour cream
or a little mayonnaise).

Wouldn't this be ideal for those leftover turkey, roast,
and ham scraps? I love it because it separates easily, even
after it freezes!


"I put boiled, peeled eggs *whole* in fruit jars, and pickle
them. Sometimes I make one jar plain with just vinegar,
one jar perhaps with pickled beet juice, and keep refriger-
ated.

"They make 'delish' salads, tangy deviled eggs and just
plain good eating."


"Here's a tip if you have leftover dips from a party.

"With the onion or garlic dip, I added just a little milk
and mayonnaise to make it thin enough to pour over a
tossed salad. It makes a very tasty and unusual dressing."

*Some Like It Cold*    161

## ❦ Just Desserts

Home at five, dinner at six, no time for a fancy dessert? That's what you think:

"For a real treat, try putting some hot chocolate pudding over vanilla ice cream! It sure is delicious."

Bake it Saturday—and eat it all week: "There are only two of us at home, but we still like homemade pies.

"When I bake pies for our freezer, I cut them in slices before freezing. Then when I want some, I just take out the number of pieces I need and don't have to thaw the whole pie! Because they have been pre-cut, the frozen pieces divide easily for quick thawing."

This little hint is for anyone who uses boxed puddings (which all say "add milk," etc.).

Put the milk in your cooking pot *first*, and let it get barely warm. Remove about a half-cup of the milk and add this to the boxed pudding and mix it well. Then pour this mixture back into the rest of the hot milk. Your pudding will thicken twice as fast. Saves standing there and stirring it so long with a spoon.

Also, did you ever try using your pancake turner instead of a spoon to stir pudding and gravy? Scrapes a larger area on the bottom of the pan, is quicker, and prevents lumps and scorching.

After years of trying to cut corners and save a few minutes, you'll just die when I tell you how to open a package of boxed pudding without breaking your fingernails, or getting mad when you try to get the last dregs out of that plastic sack inside. This is also good for cakes, gelatin desserts, and just about anything that comes in a box.

Instead of trying to open the ends, lay the box flat and

using a sharp knife, cut that box almost in half as if you were slicing bread. Cut only through the top and two sides, leaving the back intact.

Now, pick up the box and hold it over your mixing bowl, then turn it upside down, and bend it backwards. Every iota of its contents will spill into your bowl with absolutely no effort whatsoever on your part!

Here's a time-saver that works for me:

"A one-pound coffee can saves me time and undue work when I prepare that new whipped dessert mix. After putting the ingredients in, I only use one beater on my mixer and it doesn't spatter at all.

"Then I put it in the refrigerator to chill right in the can."

And here are two good ones for gelatin lovers: "Here's a tip for making individual gelatin molds:

"After you have used all the margarine in one of those soft margarine tubs, don't throw it away. Wash it out, and the next time you are making gelatin, just lightly grease the tub, and fill it to the top with gelatin.

"Let it chill, and after it has completely jelled, run warm water over the bottom for a couple of seconds. Presto, you have a beautiful mold, just as pretty as anyone can buy."

"I was making gelatin and wanted to give some to our new tenants upstairs who have children. So I let the gela-

tin cool thoroughly, then poured it into paper cups which I had set in a pie tin and put them into the refrigerator.

"There was no worry about returning dishes, or taking the chance of a child breaking one, when this 'goody' was put in paper cups. Moreover, the children loved the colored paper cups!"

This would be a good after-school snack for little tots, too! Mothers wouldn't even have to wash the cups.

## ❦ Candy Capers

I have been experimenting lately with chocolate fudge recipes (especially ones that call for marshmallows) and have found a fantastic way to make one batch of it into three different flavors with no extra pots, pans, or effort:

Set aside three little cake pans to pour your batter in *before* you even start cooking your fudge. Line each pan with plastic wrap. (It will not stick to teflon.)

As soon as your fudge is ready to pour, put only one-third of it in the first pan.

Add three heaping tablespoons of dry powdered cocoa and one tablespoon of imitation brandy extract (cherry or orange flavors are also excellent) to the rest of the mixture. Stir it quickly until it completely dissolves and pour some more in the second pan. This will give you a *dark*, bittersweet fudge with a taste all its very own.

Now, you're left with one-third of your fudge. The last is the very best of all and will make such a great concoction that you'll wonder where your original recipe went!

Quickly sprinkle three big spoons (according to the size recipe you're using—I use a big one) of instant coffee on the remaining fudge. *Add nothing else.* Mix well and dump this into your last pan.

You've got the most delicious bittersweet-coffee fudge you ever shook a stick at.

You'll absolutely drool. Wonderful for after-dinner desserts and at parties. And why not take a batch to the office? Just think: Three different kinds of candies came out of one recipe with very little extra effort on your part.

A super tip for easy melting: "Do you find it hard to melt baking chocolate when making candy, icings, or cakes?

"When I buy a bar of it, I grate the whole bar on the smallest grater, then place it in a tightly sealed jar. This way my grater has to be cleaned once and the chocolate is ready for use any time. You'll be surprised how much time this saves."

### ☙ Hey, Cookie

Save your empty waxed paper and foil boxes.

Line them with either wax paper or foil, dump in your excess cookie dough, and whack (that means slam the box down) on your drainboard. The dough will adhere perfectly to the shape of the box. Naturally, you're going to have a square cookie! But they're cute!

You can keep this in your refrigerator for as long as a week and then take it out, slice them and cook them. If you have a freezer, they will keep indefinitely.

I also learned that instead of slicing them real thin with a sharp knife, you could slice them thick—as much as a

quarter of an inch—and then cut that slice in fourths with a sharp knife.

You can also save your frozen fruit juice cans. After all, you have only cut the top off. Pack your cookie dough into these and put in your freezer.

The next time you want to bake some cookies on a small scale, remove the number of cans you want and cut out the bottom end, but do not remove it. Use this disk to push the dough out of the can.

### ❦ Tall and Cold

"Here's a tip if you are having a party and want to serve cold drinks in fancy, frosted glasses. Fill the glasses with hot water from the faucet, then pour it out and quickly put the glasses in the freezer for a least thirty minutes before using.

"When you take them out they will frost up and make the drinks look cool and refreshing."

Have you ever tried frosting the edge of the glass? All you need is a thin paste of powdered sugar and lemon juice in a shallow bowl. Turn each glass upside down, twist the edge in the paste, and then freeze.

This will make a delicious frosty lemon ring all around the edge of your glass that will last until that tall glass of tea or lemonade is all gone.

Try lime and concentrated orange juice, too. Sure makes your guests think you've gone to a lot of trouble, and it only takes a minute.

"I put some lemon juice in the water when I make ice cubes. These are excellent for use in iced tea and other drinks."

"Did you know that when you put a six-pack of canned soft drinks in your refrigerator, if you remove the cans from the cardboard carton, they will get cold faster?"

A tomato with a few slices taken off . . . or a half lemon or orange will keep perfectly for days if the cut side is turned *down* on a plastic coffee can lid.

You can take tangerine, orange, or grapefruit sections apart and freeze them. Makes a cool refreshing treat, especially for little kiddies.

After peeling a cucumber, scrape it lengthwise with the prongs of a sharp salad fork. This makes beautiful indentions. Then slice crosswise. Very decorative.

All you gals who have blenders, remember to use them for making quick, grated cabbage slaw. Wowie! Fill the jar half-full of cold water and put chunks of cabbage in. Slap the top on and quickly turn the blender on and off a few times.

Pour the contents into a strainer and mash the excess water out. Can be squeezed dry with your hands. Instant slaw with no effort at all!

"When I want to use just a portion of a head of cabbage I first remove and set aside one or two of the outer leaves that I need. Then I cut off the amount of cabbage that I am going to use. I take the outer leaves that I've set aside and use them to seal the cut side of the head of cabbage to be stored.

"I never have discolored cabbage this way, because there is enough moisture in those leaves to retain the freshness on the cut side."

I do suggest wrapping it in a piece of plastic wrap if it's going to be a week or so before you finish using the rest.

Know that leftover cherry juice you've all got on the

refrigerator shelf? Here are a few ideas for putting it to use.

Next time you fix some of that fabulous dessert topping (low-calorie whipped cream), try pouring that little bit of juice in to substitute for part of the milk called for in the recipe. It's absolutely *the most!*

Also try a spoonful of red or green cherry juice dribbled over a grapefruit half. It will run along those tiny tributaries and add a touch of interest to plain white grapefruit.

And for little ones who are allergic to chocolate, some of that cherry juice in their milk is a true delight.

If you're sick of buying ice cream and having it become slushy in the freezing compartment of your refrigerator, pay heed to this advice.

The best thing I found outside of putting ice cream in an ice tray and covering it with foil or plastic wrap to prevent frost, is to transfer it to those little empty margarine tubs you've been saving, as soon as you bring it home from the store. Then clamp the lids on and store the tubs in your freezer compartment. My ice cream stays nice and firm then.

And another thing, when you're watching TV at night and decide to eat ice cream, you don't dirty a bowl. Just let your loved ones pick up a tub, grab a spoon out of the drawer, and eat away.

Some of us hesitate to make potato salad very often because we have to drag out so many bottles and spices to season it with, that it's just too much trouble. Here's an easy way for you.

I use a large bowl and always take four times the amount of the salad dressing mixture I need at one particular time. This includes the mayonnaise, chopped pickles, pimentoes, vinegar, onions, mustard, savory salt, celery salt, salt, pepper, and always a few drops of yellow food coloring. The yellow coloring makes it look like you've got lots of boiled eggs.

I use what I need to make my potato salad that day, pour the rest in a pint jar, and keep in my refrigerator. This will keep for months.

If you follow this idea . . . the next time you make potato salad, all you have to do is boil your potatoes, dump some of your favorite mixture in and add that hard-boiled egg.

Anytime I boil my potatoes for a salad, I always drop an egg or two in the same pan of boiling water. Saves washing an extra pan.

## ✨ Save Catsup

Another cutie pie has a wonderful idea:

"My husband has an excellent way to empty catsup bottles that's real thrifty. He learned it while working in a restaurant.

"You simply put your almost empty catsup bottle upside down on the top of a new bottle. (With both tops removed, naturally.) If necessary, balance it between some boxes or canned goods.

"In a little while every single drop of the catsup will flow into the new bottle. No waste and not at all messy. It cleans itself completely up to the neck of the bottle."

Here's a hint that may help someone who, like myself, just hates to shred cabbage for coleslaw. I use a cabbage shredder (the flat kind), but always seem to get more cabbage on the counter than in the bowl.

With the vegetable peeler, more goes into the bowl! Most amazing thing you ever saw. And oh, so easy.

I found it better to quarter the cabbage, lay one cut side down and start shredding from the exposed cut side at a 45-degree angle. The slices turn out paper thin and uniform.

I then put it in a bowl and cover it with ice water so it would be crunch-crisp by suppertime. Shake the water off and put your dressing on and it's fit for Queen Elizabeth. And *don't* forget the celery seed. I even put thin slices of celery in mine!

Make use of that milk or buttermilk carton whenever you make pancake batter. Pour the batter back into an empty milk carton through the open spout. You can then rinse all your utensils before they become encrusted with dry, hard-to-wash-off batter.

Now pour your pancakes from the spout on the milk carton. When you are finished cooking, pinch the spout shut, and any unused batter will keep in your refrigerator. A vigorous shake mixes the batter the next day with no drippy mess . . . pancakes without even using a spoon or ladle.

When you get to the bottom of a jar of mayonnaise or salad dressing, instead of scraping it clean with a spatula, pour in some leftover sweet pickle juice, some salad oil, and some catsup. Don't measure ingredients—just pour what "feels" right!

Put the lid back on and shake vigorously. It makes a delightful dressing for tossed green salad.

I've a new way to stuff celery. First you stuff the celery, *then* you cut it into smaller pieces.

If you live where the salt gets damp in a salt shaker,

put a glass over the shaker when not in use. It will keep the salt dry and prevent it from caking.

For very crisp sweet onions: Slice, place in fruit jar, cover with cold water, and cap. Put in refrigerator overnight or longer. Change the water once if the onions are strong. Drain them on a paper towel when ready to use.
Great for salads or hamburgers.

Whenever you buy cheese, cut it into sections that will fit into a quart jar. Cap the jar tightly and put it in your refrigerator. Cheese stays fresh for a long time and doesn't dry out.

Wet a paper towel and place it over the top of leftover meats to put in the refrigerator. No dry hard edge (or top) on the meat when you slice it cold for the next meal.

Empty a can of kidney beans into a strainer. Run cold water over them until all the bubbles wash away. Then put the beans into a jar and season with salt, pepper, and garlic salt. Now, cover completely with *garlic* or *wine* vinegar. Screw on the lid and store them in your refrigerator.
When you make a mixed green salad and wish to add color and tang, add a few of those beans. Sure gives it a nice tart taste.
When you use all the beans, open another can and repeat

the process, adding just enough of the same type vinegar to cover them again. The vinegar mixture can be used repeatedly.

I find the beans are a godsend for color when tomatoes are the price of gold nuggets.

And another "budgeteer" had this idea: "I found it terribly expensive to buy green peppers out of season.

"So when the peppers are in season and plentiful, I buy some, dice them up, and spread them out on a cookie sheet, and then freeze. After they are completely frozen, I put them in a freezer container with a lid.

"Later, I can take out just as many pieces as any recipe calls for and they don't stick together. Sure is nice to have green peppers for seasoning all the year round."

And at your beck and call!

Please don't throw away the seeds! They are wonderful to put in homemade chili, dips, spaghetti sauce, swiss steaks, etc.

When you make a gelatin salad or dessert, line your mold with one of the new plastic wraps. Then there's no need to melt half the salad when you run the container under the hot water faucet.

Just take the gelatin from the refrigerator, invert it on a plate, lift off the mold or pan, and peel away the plastic liner. Presto—a perfectly molded gelatin.

One sweet gal gave us this method of freezing ground beef:

"I put one pound of ground beef inside a large plastic bag (the kind that comes in a roll) and pound it flat with the palm of my hand.

"Then I take my rolling pin and roll it until the meat

fills the area of the bag to about two inches from the opening. I fold over the flap to seal it and place it in the freezer on a flat surface. "The advantages are:

"It freezes very quickly, being wafer-thin, and retains its fresh red color. Also, it will thaw equally fast and as much or as little as you need can be broken off easily.

"Several pounds can be stored this way in thin layers. Try it, it's better than freezing ground beef in the pound chunks."

And a tired mommy offers this suggestion: "Frequently I had five or six boxes of various cereals that were less than half-full and took up a lot of cupboard space.

"Now I empty the contents of each box into a large one, then close the top, and shake. Not only saves shelf space, but gives us a new kind of interesting cereal!"

And another smart "cookie" says:

"For years I had been plagued with stains and odors in my plastic containers when storing foods such as tomato and spaghetti sauces, chili, or onions.

"The answer is to insert a plastic bag before putting the food in . . . This is especially good when thawing frozen food, because the bag slides out of the plastic container easily. It also saves scrubbing and soaking the containers."

# Chapter 12

# Some Like It Hot

Sweetie, it seems like your work is *never* done. Working gal, laundress, mother, and cook too! Sometimes I wonder how we do it. But then I think of all the wonderful little short cuts we have, and the clever ways we find to save money—without it showing. Yes—it's possible to save and

at the same time serve your dear ones *hot,* nourishing, tempting meals.

To be sure of saving on grocery bills, *never* go to the

market hungry! Always shop immediately after a meal. You gals who work close to home might try shopping after your lunch break.

With your stomach filled, you will not be nearly so temped to buy condiments, luxury items, and fancy foodstuffs! When hungry, you go for goodies to "tide you over" until dinner. If you aren't hungry, and especially if you "just can't eat another bite," they don't even tempt you! It's all psychological, but it works as a money stretcher, instead of a tummy stretcher—remember that.

Never worry about the price of necessities. Everybody must pay rent, taxes, and buy necessary foods. Accept the fact that you cannot escape these costs. Save your "worry time" for the things you buy and don't need!

We all know we need milk, flour, sugar, eggs, and potatoes! Even coffee or tea. But it's the splurges that run up our grocery bills. I have had my own family say, "This is the best ham! Why don't we have it more often?"

I always answer, "Just enjoy it, dears," and I laugh to myself. No family understands that ham costs more than hamburgers! I know we can't afford a center-cut slice of ham too often, but monotony is what gets you down.

Buy that slice of ham once a month. We need to splurge once in a while. Enjoy it when you do, and *never* feel guilty when you eat it. Why should you? Your family won't feel guilty. They'll leave the table, their tummies full, and settle down to read the paper or watch TV.

You will be out doing the dishes. That's the time to think about that wonderful slice of ham. It *helps!* And remember, that slice of ham will cost less than all the fancy foodstuffs you might have bought if you had been hungry when you went to the market.

Save this way: Serve the ham with rice or grits, ham gravy (make with water: it's so much less fattening), and a salad. Serve a gelatin dessert to make up for the extra pennies you spent on the ham.

If you need something, buy it. If it's not necessary—then *check* that *price*. But never upset yourself over things you can do nothing about.

Never take anyone with you when shopping if you can possibly help it. You don't save anything by sharing a ride to the grocery store with a friend. She'll only remind you to buy lots of goodies you *don't need* and to try the wonderful brand of olives she uses! Go shopping alone even if you have to go in a taxi.

Buy your meat *first*. Buy a week's supply at a time because if you don't, you will find that each time you go back to the store for meat, you will pick up several other things that you *could* have done *without*.

After buying your meat, buy your dairy products. Always be extravagant on eggs, oleo, and cheese. These are used for all meals and are wonderful food stretchers. Try using oleo for frying. Sometimes it is less expensive than shortening. Compare the prices *per pound*.

Never run out of potatoes. They can be cooked many ways and taste good with anything.

Set aside so much a week for groceries. Be sure it's really spent for food. Cigarettes, school supplies, aspirin, drinks, and cough syrup are *not* food.

To test this, go into the store some day and buy *nothing* except food. *Then* go back through the store and buy those other things. You will find that the real demon in that basket is not what you eat!

If you have a freezer, buy pies, meats, vegetables, and anything when it's on sale. When day-old bread is on sale, buy this too, and freeze it. (Have you ever thought the very loaf of bread you bought yesterday *is* one day old?

Go look right now and see how fresh that still is!) Day-old bread is much cheaper.

In one year's time you probably will have saved enough money on groceries to pay for your freezer. We did!

## ☞ Hot Buckets

When two members of a family work, you usually have to double those times when a hot meal will have to stay hot while waiting to be eaten: I hope the folks who have those insulated metal ice buckets don't just save them for ice alone. They're wonderful for keeping food hot for hours.

"When I cook I wrinkle up a piece of foil, then slightly straighten it out again—leaving it real crinkly so that it looks kind of like a waffle.

"When I lay fish sticks on this to bake, both sides of the sticks get crisp at the same time because the heat gets in the little crinkles and they never stick."

## ☞ Cereal For All

You gals who have to dash out in the morning for work will like this idea:

"Here's a hint for those who like hot cereal in the morning—that can be prepared right after supper the night before.

"Fill a wide-mouthed vacuum bottle with hot water, put in the cork and set the bottle aside. Cook your hot cereal thoroughly. Instead of pouring it in your bowl (as you would ordinarily the next morning), pour the water out of the thermos and put the cereal in the bottle!

"Cork and cap the bottle firmly and lay it on its side on a towel (so it won't roll) on the drainboard. That's all there is to it. In the morning you will have a hot, thoroughly cooked bowl of cereal ready in an instant."

And these tempters are sure to keep your little ones from dawdling in the morning while *you're* trying to get out:

"I save all the extra syrup that comes from my canned fruits such as pineapple and peaches and pour it in a syrup pitcher. I put this in my refrigerator.

"Each morning when my children eat cereal—which they dearly love—after they pour on their milk, they top it with this canned syrup juice.

"Sure lessens the sugar content. Besides, it changes the taste of nearly every cereal. How's about that for trying to save a dime and making your family happy?"

"I have seven children who love hot cereal but they get tired of it just sugared and with raisins.

"One day I hit on the idea of putting the bowls of cereal on the table with packages of chocolate and strawberry powder which are normally used to flavor milk.

"Did they go for it! Now they just spoon on whichever flavor they want (yes, they sometimes mix them!) and everybody is happy."

### ❦ Pancake Delights

"I save leftover breakfast pancakes and fix them a delicious way! I spread each pancake with jam or jelly, roll it up, fasten with a toothpick, and dip it in or sprinkle with confectioners' sugar. Then I stack them on a plate in the refrigerator ready for the 'raiders.' "

"Have you ever tried serving children their pancakes in a wide, shallow soup plate? It sure keeps most of the syrup on the pancakes and not on the table."

### ✌ *Toast Treats*

Even a busy working mother has time for these easy ways to spice up the breakfast toast:

"Do you love cinnamon toast but hate the mess? Try creaming your butter, cinnamon, and sugar all together and then spread it on the hot toast."

A right neat trick! The cinnamon and sugar stay on top of the toast where they *belong*.

"I mix my sugar and cinnamon by the pound for my four eager eaters and put it in an empty salt box that has both the spout and sprinkle opening. This way it's always ready for toast."

"Try putting granulated gelatin (strawberry is what my children like best) on hot buttered toast. Take the gelatin in its dry form, place it in an empty shaker, and sprinkle it over the toast. Delicious! It's a welcome change from cinnamon toast."

I have an idea I know your kids will love. You know those packages of powdered drink mixes you buy which come in grape, orange, strawberry, etc.? Well, instead of plain old cinnamon toast for breakfast, try using some of this. It's absolutely the greatest.

Many of you working gals don't have very large families to cook for. I'll bet you're often faced with recipes that call for just a little bit of something—meaning plenty of waste. I'll bet too many of the foods you like are both perishable and sold in quantities too large for your needs.

Bacon, for instance, spoils easily: "Here's a good breakfast tip.

"To prevent a pound of bacon from becoming rancid before it can be used, fry the whole pound at once, drain it on paper, and put it in a wide-mouthed glass jar in your refrigerator.

It will be all ready to just pop under the broiler for a minute when getting breakfast. You will save time as well as bacon this way."


Are you all forever needing a little diced or crumbled bacon for a recipe? Seems like I am. One day I needed some for a recipe and had to get out a new pound of bacon. While opening the package, I got a terrific idea.

I picked up my butcher knife and whacked about a half an inch off both ends of that whole pound of bacon. Perfect! I used what I needed for my recipe, put the rest in a waxed bag and stored in my freezer for future use.

So gals, when you bring home that pound of bacon from the grocery store, open the package and whack some off the ends before you ever put it away. But if you don't have time right then, you can do it easy as pie after it has been frozen. I do.

Your family is going to eat that two (or maybe three) slices of bacon each morning anyway, no matter how long the slices are. They won't even miss those little tidbits you got on the sly! It sure is handy and saves time when you're in a hurry (and aren't we always).

When you want a few slices of onion but don't need a whole one, *don't peel it before* you slice it. Leave that peel or skin on the onion and go ahead and slice it. Then just take your fingernail or your fingers and lift off that *outside* peel from those slices! It's twice as quick.

Also I've learned that you do not have that onion odor left on your hands! The dry peel protects your hands from odor.

If you only use half of the onion and still have the peel on the outside, all you have to do is put it on a saucer or a piece of plastic and lay it with the cut side down in your refrigerator. God put that ol' skin on the outside of the onion for a reason, didn't He? I think I finally figured out what it is!

A sweet woman once told me to buy a box of whole, mixed pickling spices. She suggested I keep it on hand in case I ever ran out of a certain spice so that I could grab the kind I wanted out of this mixture in emergencies.

Well, I did and it has been a lifesaver. Once in a while I run out of bay leaves, clove, whole black pepper, chilies, etc. All I have to do is pick out the spice I need from the mixed spices.

The brand I bought has eleven different spices in it. This would be especially good for new brides just starting in housekeeping or for small families who don't use a lot of spices.

Since it all comes in one box there won't be eleven different jars or cans cluttering up the cabinet. Might try buying a box next time you're grocery shopping. It's not expensive and sure comes in handy.

### ❦ The Gravy Train

"After I empty a can of vegetables into the pan, I just set the can aside. When making the thickening for my gravy, I mix it in the same can—and I have no dishwashing!"

### ✿ Breading

"I work in a restaurant. When they do any breading of fish, chops, or vegetables with cracker crumbs, they roll a package of crackers real fine, and add one-fourth to one-third cup of flour and mix them together well.

"Then they bread the meat by pressing it into the crumb-and-flour mixture and shaking off the excess. It handles easily without any mess. I make this breading mixture all the time at home and keep it on hand. Saves buying cracker crumbs already prepared, and is far less expensive."

You can try this in your blender, gals. Use *no salt*. That's already on the crackers, remember?

### ✿ Stretch Your Good Eating

We're all interested in ways to stretch pork chops, veal cutlets, rib-eye steaks, and the like. I just learned a terrific way to do this so that it will stretch for more than one person.

Take your pounder (that's the little gadget you buy at your dime store). And, for goodness sake, if you don't have one, go buy one (they cost less than a dollar), and mash or beat on that little rib-eye steak, deboned pork chop, or chicken until it's flat. I usually put my meat down on the piece of plastic it came in, and do my beating on that.

The meat will expand to about twice the original size.

Furthermore, every time you beat it with the pounder (using the little, pointed ends) you break up any tough connective tissue and make it even more tender.

Another thing I learned was that after pounding the meat, folding it over and pounding it more, I could take a sharp paring knife, and cut the meat into squares (these will not really be squares, but hunks of meat), then fry them.

And don't think these aren't good in place of meatballs and spaghetti! They make a luscious dinner when chicken-fried, steamed in gravy, and poured over a pound of rice or noodles! It's out of this world.

## 🐝 How to Thaw

Let me put a little bee in your bonnet about how to thaw steaks, chops, and anything in the meat line. When you

take meat out of your freezer in the frozen state, *don't* remove the wrapper to let it thaw quickly. This ruins good meat. I'm not talking about hamburger. I'm talking about roast, steaks, and chops.

In the morning, remove whatever meat you are going to cook that night, leave it in its original wrapper, then wrap it in about three sheets of newspaper. Along about dinner time the meat will have slowly thawed. You will find much less blood has escaped and you will have a much juicier piece of meat when cooked.

## 🐝 Frying Well

While you all are frying that good chicken, have you ever thought to fry some potatoes in the skillet at the *same* time? Sure makes for good eating.

Also, fried potatoes need not be peeled. Wash and dry them with a paper napkin and continue from there.

Want to know how to keep butter from burning in a skillet when pan-frying a steak? Here is what I learned from a famous French cook: Always put a wee bit of vegetable oil in the bottom of your skillet first. As soon as it gets hot, then put your dabs of butter in. This way the butter floats on top of the oil, bubbles up (and mixes beautifully), and browns gently without ever burning. How about that?

### ❦ Stew Party

Working gal, divvy up that cooking (just as you did your housework). This "Stew Party" is a real fun way to save time.

"Call your neighbors and ask them over for a 'Stew Party.' Have each one bring her leftover vegetables, meats, etc., or anything on hand that goes in to make a good stew.

"When it's all pooled, it makes a batch large enough for the whole crowd. And boy is that stew ever good! Don't know why, but it tastes so much better than if you had stayed home and prepared it just for your own family out of your own leftovers.

"Besides, it's a good way for everyone to get rid of those leftovers and have an enjoyable time doing it.

"I did this in my neighborhood recently and it was such a 'hit' that I thought others might like to hear of my idea. It was so much fun and practically no cost to any one of us either."

A good name for this fantastic idea is a bring-what-you-have party!

### ❦ The Burger Beautiful

In a café one day I had some hamburger meatballs that had been baked and a thick cheese sauce poured over them. It was a lovely dish, but the most surprising part of it all was when I cut into that meatball with my fork, there was melted cheese on the inside too! The cook had put a small square of cheddar cheese in the middle before cooking them. As he baked them in the oven (375 degrees), the inside cheese had melted. Way out on that cloud nine, I'd say.

Something different from the regular old meatballs. If you don't want a cheese sauce poured on top, any tasty thick sauce would be a welcome change.


What's that old saying about "Who forgot the mustard?" Anyway, folks, on a recent picnic I forgot it. Now, what's a hamburger without *mustard?*

We did happen to have some bottled barbecue sauce which one usually puts on chicken and steaks, so I used that. 'Twas wonderful! I've never heard of a barbecued hamburger, but since that forgetful day, we have them all the time.

The sauce may be applied as you cook the meat over the grill or just poured on top of the meat after it is pan-fried. I found you could get more of that delicious tasting sauce on the sandwich if you would also pour it on the bun itself.

Sure does change the taste of the old, ordinary hamburger. So why not try scrumptious Bar-B-Cue Burger?


"For those who are on diets and absolutely have to have some delicious hamburger but don't want all the calories in a big thick hamburger bun: Try using the heels from a loaf of bread to put that goody in!

"My wife keeps a plastic bag in the freezer and puts the heels from every loaf of bread into it. Now when we have hamburgers, we use those heels! It is foolish to throw them away, and I can bet that most families do just that."

"When frying hamburger patties, I place a piece of aluminum foil on top of the meat and then put my open buns on top of that. There is enough room for the steam to get up to the buns and make them fresh as can be.

"So by the time the meat is cooked, the bread is piping hot. No need for sogginess due to buns placed directly on the hamburger meat."

### ❦ Spaghetti for Purse and Palate

This exciting idea is not only for those who are on tight budgets, but also for those who just love spaghetti with meatballs or meat sauce. The main complaint I have gotten from husbands is, "My wife always serves spaghetti, and it's so colorless and unappetizing."

When I was boiling spaghetti one night, after putting salt and a little oil in the water, it dawned on me, "Why can't this look like egg noodles—so rich-looking and yellow?"

So I picked up my bottle of yellow food coloring, and poured in ten drops of the food coloring. After all, I couldn't lose anything but a box of spaghetti.

I could not believe that the coloring would actually soak into the spaghetti itself, and make it the rich, beautiful color of our homemade egg noodles. But you know what? It did!

It was the most luscious, egg-colored spaghetti you have ever seen in your life. It looked like it was made from pure butter and eggs.

So, gals, next time you cook some spaghetti—it works with egg noodles, and that plain old white macaroni too— please put a little bit of yellow food coloring in it. You'll be surprised how appetizing it looks—the psychological effect is most amazing!

Be sure to pick up that little bottle of yellow food coloring. It's one of the least expensive things you can purchase for your household today and it isn't loaded with calories.

Here are two tasty ways to give leftover spaghetti and sauce the respect they deserve:

"Here's a hint we learned when we were in the restaurant business. To be able to keep leftover spaghetti and macaroni, do not add your sauce but serve it separately. Then any leftover spaghetti or macaroni can be placed in a bowl of cold water and stored in your refrigerator.

"When you wish to use it, drain, and put it in boiling water only long enough to heat thoroughly. It's as good as fresh cooked when that good hot sauce is poured over it. And so convenient."

"When I have some leftover spaghetti sauce but not quite enough for another meal, I boil some pinto or kidney beans, add the spaghetti sauce, and some chili powder, and presto—instant chili."

"Here is an easy and different way to fix hamburgers: Take a square pan and just put your meat in, patting it down all around the pan. Put it under the broiler and when done on one side, cut into squares, flip over, and let cook on the other side.

"Use bread slices instead of buns and see how your family goes for 'squareburgers.' Sure saves time making those patties."

If you've got some leftover wieners and mashed potatoes and really want something splendiferous . . . Plop some of those cold 'taters on top of your wieners (split length-

*Some Like It Hot*     187

wise almost through). Then slip them under the broiler to warm up. Just as those 'tater tops start to brown, slide out your pan and put a bit of grated sharp cheese over them. Then return to oven until cheese has melted.

Sprinkled with paprika it's really a meal-in-one and ever so economical. A little chopped onion and/or parsley will add extra flavor to the potatoes.

You can pour maple syrup in a pie plate and dot with butter pats, then scatter a few pecans on top. Place your canned biscuits over the pecans and bake away. Turn them over to serve for breakfast.

And don't forget you can always cut them in fourths and deep fry them. Sprinkle on sugar and you have some mighty good eating in nothing flat. These fry quickly, so watch them.

Leftover toast can be used for French toast, and is far tastier and not as soggy in the middle.

After chopping vegetables or onions on your cutting board, it's far easier to pick them up if you use your pancake turner to scoop them up.

If you prop up one leg of your electric fry pan (set it on the handle of a dinner knife) you can make relatively grease-free hamburgers by frying them on the high side.

Using this same method you can fry bacon on one side while you fry your eggs on the "down" side where your fat has collected.

Never throw away the outside peelings from onions when barbecuing or frying hamburgers or steaks on an outside grill.

When the coals die down a bit, throw all the onion peels on top of them. It will give off such a heavenly odor that everybody will get hungry.

Want a change in those scrambled eggs for breakfast? Cook your bacon real crisp and crumble it into small pieces. Dump into your partially scrambled eggs and finish cooking.

There are about a hundred ways to make bean sandwiches. They can be made open-faced, which means one piece of bread with hot beans poured directly on top, and then go from there, or . . .

Close-faced, which means you can use two pieces of bread, a hamburger bun, English muffins, etc., and put a top on it and hold it in your hands when you gobble it up. Usually these are made from leftover beans, or any kind of beans your family has a hankering for.

On a hot open sandwich, the beans are not mashed. You just put down a piece of bread or toast, pour the hot beans over it, sprinkle on some chopped onions, dash some catsup or hot sauce over that, sprinkle grated cheese over the top of that, and top with a dash of paprika.

This seems to be the favorite, but you can ad-lib from the beans on up—dictated by your own little taste buds.

The closed sandwich is usually made on hamburger buns. You heat any leftover beans (the canned Mexican Chili Beans and Pork and Beans are wonderful) and using your potato masher, mash them as if you were mashing potatoes. They will end up just about the right consistency. Spread this on the hot bun. (Down around Texas way, people break up corn chips and mix with the mashed beans. This is a real crunchy "bit.")

This closed type of sandwich usually has a piece of thin

cheese laid on top of the beans (grated can be used, and I find it better), a thin slice of tomato, split onion rings, hot sauce, and chili sauce or catsup, shredded lettuce . . . and is topped with a hamburger patty.

Then the top of the bun is put on! The fun is trying to get your choppers over it. It's out of this world.

All of you budgeteers can make up your own sandwich to fit your taste buds. If your name is Mary, why not call it Mary's Sandwich? You will be surprised how teen-agers love them. I guess it doesn't matter what they call it as long as it's inexpensive, filling and helps on the budget.

Let's talk a bit about potatoes.

Most everybody loves mashed, smashed, or whipped potatoes—besides they are inexpensive. So, we will probably continue to use them. As far as I am concerned, there is nothing better than keeping a box of instant potatoes in our cupboards. The day you reach into the potato bin and find your potatoes pithy or soft with eyes, and can't use them, you can always reach for that emergency box of instant potatoes.

Now, here's the switch. Plain mashed potatoes and gravy? Nothing doing. Let's change it a bit and pep it up.

I happened to spy a box of dehydrated onions that I also always keep for emergencies, and thought, "Now, Heloise, put your thinker to work and figure out some way to vary plain old mashed potatoes." I tried three ways, but here's the most successful which we find absolutely delicious.

The directions on the box will say to use so-much water for so-much potatoes. I added two tablespoons of extra water and dumped a tablespoon of chopped, dehydrated onions in the water and let it sit about ten minutes.

Then I brought the water to a boil with the onions in it,

added the salt and oleo (or butter), and continued following the directions on the box.

Gals, this will give you a crunchy bite when you eat those mashed spuds and the onions also season them. Why don't you try this? Guests will love it as much as your own family. For those extra special occasions, top that dish of Heloise's onion-potatoes with some finely grated cheese. It melts in a jiffy and is delicious.

"When you have frozen dinners, save the aluminum foil from the top of the trays, wash it and use it to wrap baking potatoes . . ."

### ✿ Baked Potatoes, Eh?

An adorable chef has this advice: "Anyone who says a potato wrapped in aluminum foil can be baked is badly mistaken!

"A potato is 87 percent moisture and will *steam* when wrapped in foil and placed in a heated oven.

"Try this sometime: Wrap one washed potato in foil. Wash, score (this means stick a knife through the skin in a few places . . . so the steam can escape, Honey Bears!) and lightly grease the skin on another.

"Then . . . bake both in the same oven at the same time.

"You will find a world of difference in the flavor of the two potatoes."

And he was right as rain! One was beautifully *baked*, flaky dry and lush, while the other *was* steamed and soggy. Since that chef told me his handsome secret, I have *never* baked a potato *any* other way. If you find you just have to have that foil on them . . . Wrap the foil around the potato . . . *after* it's baked!

Here's a hint for stretching bacon. Flour is good, but have you tried dipping each strip into a mixture of one-part yellow corn meal to two-parts flour, *then* frying?
I have! It's double-good and you really have something to show for your money.

To prepare a quick and easy meal for your family, use a can of prepared biscuits, roll them out, and wrap them around wieners. Place on a cookie sheet, pop into the oven, and cook until the biscuit part is crisp.
Children love them with mustard or catsup—chopped onions.

And another hint from a gentleman:
"When I ran a café, I used to make the best French fried onion rings in town. I dipped the onion rings in a batter made from a prepared pancake mix, and had no measuring or sifting to do.

### ꙮ Meat Loaf—The Good Old Stand-by!
When all else fails (including your brain and budget!) and the prices of other meats are the cost of gold inlays . . . remember hamburger, and let's make a meat loaf.
Speaking as a working woman, let me say that one should never make one loaf at a time. Always make at least two. You can freeze one of them uncooked, cooked completely, or partially cook it and then freeze. I like the

last way the best because on our "tired days" it takes less time to cook if we are in a hurry. And just who isn't nowadays?

Meat loaf is great when served hot the first night with baked potatoes (and always throw in a few extras because they can be pan-fried or used for making potato salad the next day). As long as that oven is going, utilize that heat at the same time. Saves more money.

The next night you can slice your loaf in thick pieces and broil under your broiler. Delicious when spread with oleo, barbecue sauce, or chili sauce. And what a change it makes for your taste buds, as it disguises the hamburger in a big way.

It can always be pan-fried quickly for either open- or close-faced sandwiches; diced and when slightly browned, scrambled with eggs for a quick hot meal, or put into that wide-mouthed thermos when you pack your lunches.

If in a hurry to cook a meat loaf some night after a hard day's work—try cooking the meat in muffin pans! Cooks real quick thataway. You can also hasten it along if, after plopping your meat-loaf in your iron skillet, you heat it on top of one of your burners a wee bit first before putting it in that oven . . . I leave the skillet (or baking dish) on top of the burner until it barely starts to "bubble," then plop it in my oven.

To vary meat loaves you can always add a package of onion soup . . . or grated carrots (which are fantastic, give color, are cheap, and make the meat go further), instead of crackers or bread. And sometimes try seasoned dressing crumbs. In one country I lived in they always add grated, raw, or leftover potatoes! That's another dilly of a stretcher.

As far as stretchers go, try farina, crushed corn-flakes, precooked or raw oatmeal—these things do *not* show after cooking. I nearly always add a bouillon cube that has been liquified with a tablespoon of hot water. Great! This can be varied by using hot sauce, Worcestershire, or a bit of chili powder.

When mixing all the glop together, try putting all your ingredients into a heavy plastic bag and blend by squeezing the mixture. Saves greasy hands and extra bowls to wash. And lots of folks use their potato mashers to mix with.

For those who are on low-fat diets and want to get rid of some of that grease that drips out of a meat-loaf, try putting the loaf on a small cake rack, then placing it in a pan. The meat will brown on all sides and the fat will drop in the pan.

And don't ever forget, as long as you're mixing the goop, make up a big amount and divide some of it into thick patties and freeze them in plastic bags. I add dehydrated onions with these separate portions—and make what they call "Salisbury Steaks." Whoever gave that fancy name to a hamburger patty had lights turned on in his cranium, eh?

And so much for America's good old stand-by. Whatever would we do without it?


For those of you who cook instant rice or anything that says, "Put the lid back on . . ."

Did you know that after you stir the contents in the pot, and put the lid back on, that if you *twist* the lid and let it spin a bit as if you were playing roulette wheel . . . that the steam from the hot water would seal the lid?

You can't possibly lift that lid without a firm pull! Try it next time.

I also find that it utilizes the same principle as a pressure cooker. Not one iota of that steamy heat will escape. And your food will stay warmer longer. How about that?

At a friend's home one night, I was served instant rice in a delicious new way. She showed me how she fixed it by bringing the water to a boil, pouring in some frozen peas (according to the amount of rice being made), bringing the water back to a boil, stirring it once with a fork, then putting in the precooked rice.

Not only did it add something green to plain white rice, but made it crunchy . . . especially yummy with gravy poured over it. The boiling water cooks the peas and after the lid is put on the rice, it steams them perfectly. Absolutely on Cloud Nine.

And if you're real cute, you'll put about five drops of yellow food coloring in that water before you dump in the rice. It looks like it's loaded with butter, makes the rice yellow and, oh, what a difference it makes!

To make quick, lumpless gravy, sprinkle instant potatoes in the hot meat juice and swish it around a few times. Besides being a nice change, it makes a very nourishing gravy.

Here's a little hint to help in the kitchen. It saves cleaning another pot and might come in handy when you are using all four burners on your stove and need one more . . . if someone in your family doesn't like rice. Before cooking rice (not instant, but the kind you simmer 25 minutes), peel one potato and cut it in quarters. Then, after you bring the water to a boil, stir in the rice and put the potato, piece by piece, gently in the water on top of the rice.

Next . . . on goes the lid, the burner is turned on simmer, and by the time the rice is done you also have a steamed potato. And the rice comes out absolutely perfect. It's never soggy because the potato takes up the extra moisture.

Another way to grab a fifth burner out of the air is to use a double boiler:

You can cook carrots (or any vegetable) in the bottom of a double boiler and dump a can of peas, etc. in the top. And remember folks, canned peas are *not* supposed to be cooked. Canned peas are only supposed to be *heated*. Never let them boil.

Have you ever tried French fried sweet potatoes? Prepare and fry the raw sweet potatoes the same as white spuds.

Corn on the cob tip: Try mixing the salt and pepper in the butter for corn on the cob. Saves time and is especially helpful for children.

Ever tried putting the pat of butter on your plate, adding the salt and pepper on top of that and then spreading it all on the corn? Three operations are done at one time.

Good surgery, in my estimation!

Anytime a recipe says "and add one or two eggs," always *separate* the whites from the yolks and beat the yolks into the mixture along with all the other ingredients.

Then beat the whites until stiff but not dry, and fold

them into the dough. (That means dump them on top and lift up the batter with your mixing spoon and keep putting it on top of the whites, mixing gently until all is well-blended.)

Your pancakes or waffles will be twice as light, twice as high and not gummy. It costs no more.

Just takes about one minute of your time. That's all. And what's a minute when you can have good, light, crispy waffles and pancakes.

A few years ago, a chef told me that if I would put two tablespoons of vinegar in the water before dumping in eggs to be poached, that they wouldn't stick. He cooks six eggs every morning in a big skillet with an inch of water using *no* salt. Do not cover. He swore to me that I would not taste the vinegar.

I've been poaching eggs in vinegar water ever since. Really, it doesn't smell and doesn't taste. And it's for true; they *don't stick.*

The best way to lift poached eggs out of the hot water is with a potato masher the kind which has a round disc with punched-out holes.

Slide it under the egg and lift—you get all of the white, and the water runs off, but the egg doesn't.

If you like real thin, crisp toast of the melba type, try taking a piece of bread and ironing it between two pieces of foil until it's brown and thin. The ironed bread can be buttered or eaten plain, and it's delicious when cold.

I use thinly sliced sandwich bread and iron it in the foil with a *hot* iron. The toast was about one-eighth of an inch thick and very hard when cold.

Many of us are on diets and cannot eat the yellows of eggs. Yet how very hungry we get for that good breakfast with some scrambled eggs.

I know how you feel. I was on a diet, too, and after four months of no scrambled or fried eggs and a longing for some, I finally figured out the answer. Don't laugh when you read how! Try it!

After you crack your raw eggs, separate the whites from the yellows. Put the amount of egg whites you want to use in a cup.

For each egg white you have in the cup put two drops of yellow food coloring. Stir the droplets of coloring among the egg whites with a fork. Do not beat them or put them in a blender unless you want solid-yellow scrambled eggs.

The point of stirring them with a fork is . . . you will end up with part yellow and part white in your scrambled eggs. As you stir the cup of egg whites with a fork, you will find there will be a thick part that the yellow will not mix with. This part will end up as the egg white when it is scrambled. The part that mixes with the coloring will turn out yellow. Pour it into your skillet and scramble away.

I did find that you need lots of salt and pepper on this. Also you could top it with hamburger relish and it was out of this world, no matter what time of the day you ate it.

Moreover, if you put it in a blender and added some baking powder, it would turn out all the same color, but it would be fluffier like an omelet. If you like eggs all the some color, you may like this method.

But it leads you to believe that you are finally eating a scrambled egg with a yolk. What price psychology?

How do some restaurants get that beautiful golden color on the outside of fried chicken? Don't wonder anymore.

You can cook the most luscious fried chicken, breaded chops, and shrimp you have ever seen by adding about ten drops of yellow coloring to the oil *before* you *start* to heat it. It seems that the yellow clings to the outside of the meat itself. Especially when you have coated the food.

Now, when you fry chicken, if you don't eat the skin (which lots of people can't do because of their diet), remove the skin first.

Soak the chicken for a few hours in salt water, then shake excess water off and immediately roll it in flour. *Nothing else.* Lay it on a piece of wax paper and then put it in your refrigerator for at least one hour. Even overnight won't hurt. Then when you put it in the luscious, yellow-tinted oil, the batter will turn a beautiful yellow, golden color. You'll think the skin has even been left on.

This also works with any kind of chops.

A useful hint for anyone having a family reunion or a cookout: Make hamburger patties and wrap each one individually in aluminum foil and put in the freezer.

When mealtime comes, just put the hamburgers in your oven or on the grill in the same foil and cook. No mess to clean up, and no burned burgers.

When you brown tiny meatballs, instead of browning them in a skillet on the top of the stove, put them in a large greased skillet and place them in the oven. Do not cover with a lid.

Set your oven at 350 degrees and in 35 to 45 minutes, depending on how brown you want them, you'll have the nicest round and brown meatballs you've ever seen.

And sometime, try dusting them with flour first. Then when you put them in your spaghetti sauce, not only does it add thickening, but the sauce *sticks* to each meatball. Great!

Noticing turkey prices in the paper reminded me that large turkeys are always the best buy. Not only is the price less per pound, but the percentage of waste per pound is also less, and the meat is usually better quality.

Of course the size of our family, stove and refrigerator often makes a twenty- to twenty-five-pound turkey impossible.

The solution: Have the butcher saw (if frozen) or cut the turkey in halves or quarters. Freeze the extra and use it when you wish.

Who said hams have to be cut crosswise? When you buy a whole ham, have the butcher cut it in half *lengthwise!*

After the ham is cooked, the bone falls right out. So, when carving, you get nice, whole slices of ham, and there is no waste since there is no cutting around the bone. I found that ham not only cooks faster when cut this way, but when the long, flat side is laid face down on the platter, it is easier to carve.

Besides, you can cook only half a ham and freeze the other part.

And speaking of ham: Did you all know that you could slice off a few thick pieces and smoke it on your barbecue grill?

Sometimes I even punch a few whole cloves down in mine. Serve with or without barbecue sauce. It sure doesn't taste like leftover canned ham!

A quick, easy, and delicious way to prepare barbecue "grilled" chicken: Just put one or more (depending on number to be served) whole fryers in your oven and bake. (Don't cook quite as long as usual.) Remove, let cool, then disjoint.

Now all you have to do is place your chicken pieces on the grill, baste with barbecue sauce and turn them over occasionally for even browning. They're done in a jiffy. Salt and pepper to taste. It's perfectly tender and done clear through every time. You know the rest—just bite into that mouth-watering treat.

I wonder if all of you who have a deep-fat fryer with a basket really know how many things they can be used for besides frying?

I remove the basket and cook delicious soups, smothered steaks, and just about anything in the fryer part. But the greatest idea of all is to use the basket for other things . . . the basket may be used in your other pots and pans. When you boil potatoes for mashing, or carrots, take the basket and put it in your regular pan, fill it with water, then place your washed vegetables inside the wire gadget part.

When the vegetables are done, instead of putting the lid on the pot and pouring all the boiling water down into your sink (which is quite dangerous), just remove the pot from the stove and put it in your sink. Then lift out the wire basket which contains all of the boiled vegetables.

Now turn on your cold water faucet (this is to prevent steam burns), and pour the boiling water from the pot down the drain. Then pour the vegetables back into your pan and mash or whip as usual!

If you don't have a deep-fat fryer with a basket, why don't you go to your dime store and buy just a wire basket with a handle which will fit some of your most-used pans, especially the one you boil potatoes and carrots in? They're not expensive.

I know you think I am telling you to throw away a few dimes, but it's not so. Just wait until you use it and you won't be without it!

When you bake that next turkey, why don't you try tearing off a piece of foil and wrapping it around the raw ends of each turkey leg *before* you bake it?

I find that this does not let the skin split near the end of the bone where it has been cut off, and it does not dry out. Besides, it looks pretty. Also, when it comes time to carve that turkey, you can grasp the foil-covered part of the leg in your hand for neater carving! And think how nice it will be when you hand it to the children—no messy little fingers there, either.

For those of us who don't believe in wasting anything, but want to save some more money and still get a little variation for our money:

What can you do with leftover ham after you are sick and tired of baked ham, fried ham, and ham sandwiches?

I always find it cheaper to buy and cook *big* hams. Never keep ham too long. When you get near this point, get out that meat grinder. Also your sharpest paring knife. Naturally, you can't get pretty slices any more, down near the bone of the ham, so cut out all the nice chunks you can —removing all the fat.

Put these chunks in a fruit jar and tightly cap it, or in a plastic bag and freeze them. Then grind all those small pieces of ham through your meat grinder. I always use the largest grinder blade for this. Don't add anything else. Jars or plastic bags are dillies for putting the ground-up parts in to store in the freezer.

Later, this is delicious for making ham salad, wonderful for lunches or ham croquettes. The greatest part about it all is that you can take a spoon and remove *any* amount of the frozen ham that you want for that day. It doesn't stick together like most frozen foods.

The chips or small chunks can be used in scrambled eggs, soups and salads (especially macaroni—either hot or cold). The bones can be boiled for soup. If you don't eat soup, let the liquid boil down and save it for making gravy.

Are you aware that there is such a thing as turkey *steaks?* For those who get tired of beef, it is quite a change. Turkey is inexpensive when compared with the price per pound of many other meats.

I always buy a big turkey and after it's completely thawed, slit the skin on one side of the breast and remove the meat carefully. I replace the skin over the turkey and bake the rest of it as usual.

The raw breast is then cut crosswise (across grain) and frozen just as if I were freezing steaks. The turkey steaks may be broiled, fried, or barbecued. Delicious, inexpensive, and different. You can strip practically a whole turkey this way and boil the leftover pieces for soups, sandwiches, salads, etc.

For variety, this is the way I cook a chicken breast:
Remove the meat from the bone and pull off the skin. Lay the meat flat on your chopping board and pound away with the larger side of your meat pounder as if it were a chicken-fried-steak patty.

Dip it in water and shake to remove any excess. Do not

wipe dry. Then dip it in flour and set aside for at least thirty minutes before frying. As soon as the bottom is brown, turn it over. Turn only *once*. This is the secret to non-greasy chicken.

Salt and pepper it when you remove it from the skillet. *Not* before. May be eaten plain or have chicken gravy poured over it.

And, did you know that if your skillet is big enough (or your family small enough), you can fry potatoes in that skillet at the time the chicken is frying? Saves another pan to wash . . . This stripped chicken breast can also be cut in strips like French fries, battered and deep fried like potatoes. So different! Both are easy to eat.

When you want to thaw steaks or chops, don't put them directly on your drainboard where they thaw slowly or remain frozen on the bottom side.

Either use a cake rack cooler or just remove a burner rack from your stove, place it on your drainboard, and lay the steaks on it. This allows the air to get under the rack for quicker thawing, top *and* bottom.

Did you ever try greasing the aluminum wrap instead of your turkey or chicken before you wrap the bird for the oven? I find it less frustrating and have a more evenly greased bird.

Now folks: Did you ever get up in the morning and while still stumbling around in the kitchen with one eye half open, take that first sip of coffee and burn the living daylights out of your tongue? Wow, does that hurt!

The way I prevent this (which, incidentally, I've been doing for years) is *after* stirring that cup of coffee—drop in an ice cube and let it float on *top*.

Do *not* stir again.

The ice will cool that first big gulp and by the time you have a few swallows, the coffee in the bottom of the cup is still hot! Sure saves a scalded tongue!

And if you keep that extra tray of ice cubes in the drip tray under the freezing compartment as we suggested, you won't even have to open a tray.

"When I make an omelet, I don't try to flip it over in the skillet. When it's cooked on the bottom and still runny on top, I pop it under the heated broiler. Watch this carefully as the top will cook in no time at all.

"All one has to do is fold it over, and each omelet is perfect. If I fill it with onions, or any other filling which takes more cooking time than the omelet itself does, I precook the filling and then sprinkle it on top of the omelet before placing under the broiler."

"I use my egg slicer to slice potatoes that have been boiled with jackets on and then peeled. Makes for a more uniform hot potato dish. Also a nice size for hash brown."

"Add one tablespoon of minced onion to dough when making crust for meat pies. Really adds to the flavor."

When you clear the table at night and want to save some vegetables that are left over, do not transfer them to a smaller bowl. Put them in a small pan (the proper size) and set it in your refrigerator.

The reason for this is you will heat the food the next day or so anyway. Then just remove the pan from the refrigerator and heat it in the same pan. This saves washing that extra bowl. I also learned that if the leftovers are in a pan you are more apt to heat and re-serve them.

Probably a lot of us have wondered how to reheat left-over mashed potatoes without scorching them.

Just wrap in aluminum foil and heat them in the oven for a few minutes. They are just as delicious as the first time, no pan to wash, and no mess either.

The way one gal saves when using high-priced coffee:

Use one-fourth *less* coffee than usual for the same amount of water. When it stops perking, remove the lid, pour out one cup of the perked coffee and pour it back through the strainer.

You'll be surprised at the results. It may be repeated, but I have never found it necessary.

For the second pot you can also leave the grounds *in* and add some instant coffee. Perk away again. Bet you can't tell the difference. I can't.

Another thing my girl friend does, is use *all* instant coffee in her percolator, and her husband hasn't caught on yet. She says it saves emptying grounds every morning, besides taking up less room in her cabinet!

Another sweet soul had this idea:

"Here is the way we make popcorn at our house. After popping it, we pour the hot popcorn into a clean paper bag, add a teaspoon of powdered cheese, a dash of onion salt, and shake. Delicious!"

Have you ever tried putting popped corn in your deep-fat fryer basket and shaking it to remove unpopped kernels? It's much easier and faster and the corn doesn't cool off as much before being served.

I buy pickles in gallon and half-gallon jars. When I get home I slice some crosswise (at about a 45-degree angle) for hamburgers, put them in a jar, and add some of the juice.

I slice others the long way for cold sandwiches, and put them in another jar with some juice. I grate about one-third of the pickles and make relish! I pack this in a small jar and add just enough juice to cover the top. If you eat a lot of hamburgers or hot dogs, try filling a jar with one-third of this grated pickle relish (kosher, dill, sour, or sweet), your favorite mustard, and thick catsup. Mix well. You will have a relish that is out of this world for all those quick hamburger or hot dog sandwiches.

A famous pickle man once told me that if the pickles you buy are not sour enough, pour off some of the juice, and just add white vinegar to them! Works too!

Red salmon costs more than pink. Pink salmon costs more than regular.

I discovered that you can add some drops of food coloring in a bit of the juice from a can of regular salmon, stir, and put in your croquette mixture and it turns your regular salmon croquettes pink or red. All according to how much coloring you add . . .

Now how's that for fooling your family?

Potatoes? They're cheap. Let's try a new way so we won't recognize them. . . .

When preparing scalloped potatoes, slice or grate them as usual and season. Then take a can of cream of chicken soup that has been diluted with milk and heated. Pour this over potatoes and bake as usual. Delicious!

"When making chili dogs for my family, I make the chili first. Then I put the wieners in the chili for the last five or ten minutes of cooking and let simmer.

"This way they absorb all that good chili flavor and are much more tasty. Give it a try and I think you will agree."

This is strictly for fresh green bean lovers. There's nothing like them when they are cooked with bacon grease, ham hocks, etc. We all know that. But while I was snapping some one night, it dawned on me that nearly every meal the Chinese prepare has a delicious dish of something sweet and sour. So when I was ready to cook the two pounds of fresh green beans, I tried something new.

I put in one level tablespoon of sugar and one table-spoon of vinegar to the water I had covered them with. Then I added one chopped onion.

After cooking them the usual time . . . you talk about lush . . . Sweet and sour green beans! Whoever heard of that before? Since then, when I didn't have any fresh green beans in the house, I opened a can of whole green beans and added the same things. They were just about as tasty as the fresh ones.

The one thing that all of you are going to ask is, what did I do with the water that came in the can of beans? I poured it off! I held the can under the faucet and rinsed off the beans before adding fresh water and the above ingredients. Sure is different.

When you bake, boil, or buy canned sweet potatoes for mashing and you want to mix them with marshmallows . . . are they stringy?

Use your electric beater to beat them for just a few min-utes like you are making a cake batter. All of the strings will collect on the beater! It's sure better than stringy sweet potatoes.

Here's a good way to get rid of the excess grease on spaghetti sauce.

By making it a day ahead, you can accomplish two things: First, you do away with most of the cooking on the following day. Second, since spaghetti sauce will taste better the following day, you are improving the flavor and paving the way for a greaseless sauce.

After it is cold, simply lift the cold, hardened grease off the top with a spoon before reheating the sauce. All that's left to do the next day is to cook your spaghetti and pour the greaseless, reheated sauce over it.

"I remove the grates from my gas stove burners and set them on the cabinet (or elsewhere) to cool pies and cakes. The air can circulate underneath, and they work just as well as cake racks."

When melting oleo to pour in pancake or waffle batter, put a little water in the pan when you heat the margarine. This prevents the margarine from browning and the water just steams off.

"I crush a piece of aluminum foil, smooth it out a little and put it in a skillet. I put my breakfast rolls or any bread I care to warm on the foil, put a lid on and turn the fire on low. Do they ever come out piping hot! Saves on gas and keeps me from washing a pan. *Anything* to save time and money."

# Chapter 13

And just what does the number 13 mean to you? Some gals say it's unlucky—others call it their lucky number!

To each her own, I always say . . . so let's get along to Chapter 14 for our busy working gals!

Heloise

## Chapter 14

# ✠ Join the Club

"What do I do when I know that I can never get my work all done? It's very depressing. Every so often I just feel like it's useless to even try . . ."

### ✠ Never Give Up

Other gals are in the same boat with you, and it hasn't sunk yet. We're with you all the way.

Many are the days when we all get discouraged about something—whether it be housework, family, or finances.

Accept the fact that body chemistry has much to do with this, so utilize your energy or happiness to get rid of those fidgets when they strike.

If it hits you at midnight and you can't sleep, why toss and turn in the bed (and perhaps keep your husband awake)? Get up and clean a closet, a pantry shelf, drag out the sewing machine and get your mending done, or bake. At least you are getting something done that you won't have to do tomorrow.

I know for a fact that things you do when this urge or surge of "something" happens, you do *twice* as well and much faster, too. Forget your complexes and don't worry about what your neighbor says. She is going through the same thing.

You aren't the only one who gets tired and depressed. We *all* do. Relax, Hon, and enjoy life because it's so much shorter than you realize.

You'll *never* get all your work done. Just top clean and get the effect. Then you can go into deep cleaning when that fidget takes over next time.

And don't set your standards so high. Bless you always . . . all of you hard-working Working Gals.

### ❦ *Hang as You Iron*

Attach a three-prong dish-towel rack to the wide end of your ironing board and you'll have a nice built-in folding hanger for small, freshly ironed items.

When you fill your trading stamp book, dampen the page instead of the stamps and apply the stamps to the page.

And a manufacturer of dishwashers tells us: "Here's a hint for housewives who complain that their electric dishwashers sometimes don't get the dishes clean.

"Many gals run a load of dishes as soon as their family leaves for school and work—or at night before going to bed. The family has already used most of the hot water from the hot water tank, getting ready. Others try and run the dishes while they are doing their laundry. This drains the hot water heater again.

"It takes awhile for the water heater to get back up to 140 to 160 degrees. We suggest that housewives go on and load their dishwashers and close the door so that the kitchen will look clean. But, do wait until the hot water tank is at its highest temperature before washing them."

So let's go test our thermostats, gals. It should read at least 140 degrees but not over 160. If you don't know where the thermostat is, ask your husband or neighbor.

What is the difference between the dull and shiny sides of aluminum foil for cooking purposes? I checked with an aluminum foil company and they said it makes absolutely no difference which side you use for cooking.

Naturally, if you are baking a potato you would want the shiny side out, for beauty. But it's not going to make your potato any tastier.

And from an apartment dweller . . .

"I live in an apartment where all the tenants have to use the same clotheslines. To distinguish my clothespins from those of the other laundry room users, I painted a mark on all of mine with red fingernail polish. Now, there is no question as to which pins are mine."

Before you wash your cotton sheet blankets or chenille bedspreads, put them in the dryer on the air-fluff setting for a few minutes. You'd be surprised how much lint is removed from them.

"I double over about six sheets of newspaper each week and put it in the bottom of my hydrator and cover it with a few sheets of paper towels. This helps absorb the excess moisture that causes faster rotting of vegetables."

"I iron in my bedroom which is next to the bathroom. After I iron the garments that go on hangers, I hang them on the shower rod until I have finished all my ironing and am ready to put them away.

This method prevents wrinkles in the clothes and saves me walking to the proper closet after ironing each garment."

### ❦ It All Goes Out

Store small amounts of leftovers in paper cups. If not used, discard container and all.

Use your tank vacuum cleaner to remove the dust and lint from heavy clothing and blankets. This is especially good for electric blankets, heavy winter coats, trouser cuffs, inside pockets, and much easier than brushing and shaking.

Here's a hint for those who wear their hair behind their ears: If you always end up with sticky ears from spraying hair spray, use the big cap from the spray can to cover your ear, then spay away . . . No sticky ears!

And this saves your hairdo, since you don't have to wash the spray off those ears. You can wash the cap easily.

And gals, if you are one of those who are fortunate enough to have a doughboard (some call it a breadboard), but it is so worn, scratched, and stained that if you had it sanded it would be too thin . . .

Why not go to a lumber yard and buy a thin sheet of plastic counter top board and have it cut the exact size of the doughboard? Or better yet (you can't possibly make a mistake this way), put the board in your car so you will have it with you the next time you are near a lumber yard. Take it in and ask *them* to cut a piece of the plastic the size you need.

When you return home, fasten the plastic piece to the top of that glorious doughboard with six or eight tiny nails. This will make a clean and neat cutting board. You will find it worth every penny you have spent.

If you ask for scrap board you will get it for about one-fourth the regular price. Even if you buy a piece that does not match the color scheme in your kitchen, it makes no difference, as the board is usually stored out of sight when not in use.

You will love your rejuvenated doughboard. Oh, how I only wish we gals could rejuvenate ourselves that easy!

Also, here's a little trick I learned: While unzippering some cushions on a sofa and chairs for dry cleaning, I found them very hard to remove because the cloth had a rubber backing. Then when trying to push the cushions back in, I found it more difficult to get them straight because the cushions were made of foam rubber.

Know what I did? I took talcum powder and dusted the rubber backing of the fabric. The cushions slid in smooth as glass.

Also, the easiest way to insert a long cushion in one of these covers is to bend the cushion itself in the middle, then insert it and straighten it out.

Keep a plastic thimble (costs less than a dime) in your coffee can! Any time you open the can to make a pot of coffee the thimble is right there. All you do is place the thimble upside down over the coffee pot stem and measure away. After you've dumped in the coffee, just drop the thimble back in the can.

Until you can go buy a thimble, you can put your finger over the stem while spooning in the coffee. It suffices, but it's not as easy.

"I always wear rubber gloves to do my housework, especially the dishes. I was spending an awful lot just on gloves since I wear them out quickly.

"So I hit on the idea of reinforcing the thumb, forefinger, and second finger by cutting off the fingers of an old pair and inserting them inside the new ones. It's amazing how much more wear I get from my rubber gloves now."

Hate sitting under that old hair dryer? Look what one adorable friend does . . . "I made a marvelous discovery the other day at the beauty parlor.

"I took my daughter's transistor radio along and used the ear plug while I was under the dryer. It was the first time I ever had this usually boring time pass so quickly and pleasantly."

You know those plastic stacked vegetable bins we buy for the kitchen? Well, I've found a new use for mine that's absolutely great. I use them on our patio to store charcoal briquettes. The number of the bins and their size depends on how much you use your charcoal grill. I use three. I stacked them up and put an old grate across the top one. Fine place to lay hot turners and odds and ends.

When we buy a ten-pound bag of charcoal, just open it up and pour it into the two lower bins. In the top one we keep all our paraphernalia—that's tongs, hamburger turner, lighter starter fluid, etc. These items are right there close at hand when we're ready to use them.

Another good thing I found out is that you can take a heavy plastic bag and put it over the whole caboodle no matter how high you stack them. If the rain hits, it doesn't matter. It's a real neat way to take care of messy charcoal and all the junk it takes to barbecue.

And always keep an old glove in your bag of charcoal briquettes. When ready to build a fire, slip the glove on, and away you go. No soiled hands. Saves soap, hand towels, and time.

And folks, any time you open a can of something with your can opener, turn the lid upside down and lay it near your stove. Remember that lid is sterile inside. There is no reason to wash it off.

The cute trick about this is when you stir that canned food with your spoon, lay your spoon on the lid, and let it drip on that instead of dirtying up your drainboard or the spoon holder. Nothing to wash.

When you do the dishes after the meal, just throw the lid away. After all, tomorrow there will be another can . . . and lid! Or at least, let's hope so.

"As my kindergartner has trouble tying his shoes, I simply removed the laces, inserted narrow elastic, and sewed the ends. Now his shoes slip on and off easily. Sure solved a big problem for him."

Another smart mother tells us: "To make it easier for my kindergarten kiddy to identify her boots, I put decals on them.

"Not only does it make it easy for her to tell which boots are hers, but it is far easier for her to tell which boot goes on which foot . . . since I put the decal on the 'outside-side' of each boot!"

When training a child and he is wearing coveralls (with a snap crotch), if you take the front and back and snap the leg over the child's shoulder, the coveralls won't fall in the commode and get damp.

And a grandmother had this idea: "To prevent soiling the carpet when small children eat, put down a large bath towel. After a meal, it's simple to shake the towel or rinse it out if there were any spills."

Some mothers who take their babies out for a stroll in buggies sack them in a pillowcase just like a bag of sweet potatoes, after wrapping them in a blanket. The pillowcase is *never* pulled up higher than the armpits so the little arms are left free to wave and flounce.

Other mothers say that instead of putting blankets over that wee one at night which he might kick off, they pull a pillowcase over his feet and safety pin it to his nightie or pajamas, being very careful, of course, that it couldn't slip up higher than his waist.

Homemade flannel pillowcases are excellent for this purpose. They can always be used later on your bed pillows.

### ✌ Turkey Platter

If you need a large platter for a turkey, but do not want to spend the money for a turkey platter, which you will use only once or twice a year—a TV tray is the answer, so said one of our angel face dolls!

"I just place a folded newspaper in the bottom of my tray and cover it with aluminum foil! The newspaper protects the tray from cuts and scratches!"

Now this is about the trickiest thing yet. I have often seen restaurants and clubs cover trays with foil for cold cuts, roasts, and so on, but never thought about using TV trays. Those of you who don't have TV trays could use a cooky sheet beautifully.

Know what? This would also work for those beautiful silver platters that sometimes get scratched when carving. So remember to cover a folded newspaper or a piece of cardboard with foil next time you serve a hot roast or large steak on your lovely silver tray. Sure will prevent those horrible scratch marks on your good stuff.

"When I have to wash clothes at the laundromat, I carry my soap powder in empty coffee cans with the plastic lids. Much better than already opened soap boxes that usually upset and spill contents on car floors."

One Gal Friday enthused: "When I was using a rubber stamp and an ink pad to stamp our return address on some envelopes, I got ink all over my fingers.

"I always have a little can of hair spray in my desk, so I just sprayed a bit on my fingers. It washed clear off!"

And gals, here are some good tips about using clothes dryers that a leading manufacturer was kind enough to tell us:

"Dryers are perhaps the least understood of all household appliances.

"Dryers restore the natural nap of a fabric. Corduroy, velveteen, and terry cloth look and feel like new only if tumbled dry. They relax wear-and-tear wrinkles in the multitude of "no-iron" garments available for purchase—not only perma-type press, but also the chemical man-made fabric and the garments with wrinkle-resistant finishes.

"Fabrics get no warmer in a dryer than they would inside your car parked in the sun on a summer's day.

"The knowledgeable shopper can eliminate a lot of ironing by choosing fabrics wisely at point of sale. If you use coin-operated laundries, choose those with multi-load dryers that have varying temperature controls. Choose the lowest setting for chemical man-made fibers, medium for perma-type press and other wrinkle-resistant cotton finishes.

"Garments that iron themselves in the dryer should be removed and folded or put on hangers *immediately* after tumbling stops.

"Because of its natural moisture content, cotton should be removed from the dryer while it *still* contains a hint of moisture. Overdried cottons have a dry, harsh, unpleasant feel.

"Items which should *not* be tumbled dry with heat are those containing rubber of foam rubber, bath mats and rugs containing modacrylic, shower curtains and other plastics, woolens labeled "handwash" and "glass fiber."

Gals, aren't clothes dryers fantabulous things? Do remember all this valuable information when using your dryer.

Let's get down to inspecting the cord on our electric mixers—bet you will find them soiled. Especially in that little groove where the two cords are connected. Dried chocolate icing, cake mixes, etc.

Never mind about that guilt complex. I had one too when I looked at mine. Try as I might, I just couldn't get that little groove clean with a wet sponge, so . . . I took a little pan of warm water and suds and being very careful *not* to get the plug in the water (leave it hanging outside a glass, pan, or fruit jar), folded the cord and let it sit in the pan of warm suds about fifteen minutes.

With a swipe of a sponge and a dry cloth, it's clean—slick as a whistle. Why not get that one little job done today before your mother-in-law calls on you and uses it?

And while you're at it, take a look at the *underneath* part of your mixer where the spatters hit! When it's in position we never see that at all.

A gal straight from heaven taught us this time-saver: "When I wash my dishes and let them drain in the dish drainer, I only put back in the cabinet those I will *not* use for the next meal. Why should any mother who has so much to do, remove, stack, and put away five heavy plates and five glasses only to have to use her energy just taking them out again for the next meal?

"Wasn't it you who said years ago, 'When you can ride, don't walk. When you can walk, don't run. When you can sit, don't stand?' I have forgotten the rest of it. Do you remember what it was?"

You didn't miss a word, hon. Surprised you remembered it all these years. The last part was, "If you can lie down, don't sit, and if you get the chance to close your eyes, why leave them open!" And I believe every word of it. Guess I was just doggoned tired the day I wrote that!

We all love your hint. Keep in mind, too, that you can take your dish drainer right to the table while you set it! That will save a few more steps.

Another brain had a bolt of lightning hit and told us this . . . "After I load the dishwasher, I take two spring clothespins and pin my dishcloth to the top rack in the washer, hanging it horizontally so it doesn't touch the dishes in the bottom rack. Then I start the dishwasher as usual.

"I never have a sour cloth anymore, and stains usually come out, too!"

When preparing an ice bucket for a party, I pour an inch of water in the bucket and freeze. Sure helps to make the ice last longer.

Quite by accident, while trying to help a neighbor clean her copper-bottom pans, I came across a new method that is slick as a whistle!

Don't wet the pan first. But turn it upside down so the bottom is looking at you. Take your kitchen salt shaker and pour a lot of salt on it. Then take a brand new soap-filled scouring pad and pour some plain old 5 percent vinegar (out of your kitchen cabinet) on the soap-filled pad. Use this to scrub-a-dub-dub with.

You'll find the most amazing thing you have seen in ages . . . Not only will it become gleaming copper again, but it will even take the burns off the bottom of the pan!

While I was at it I also cleaned inside the same way and it did not seem to hurt it one iota. So "happy gleaming" on the bottom of your pots and pans, gals . . .

Sometimes we have extra plastic shower curtain hooks lying around (and if not, go buy some or ask your neighbor to split a package with you—this way it only costs half as much). I put some on the inside of my shower curtain between the folds and they make wonderful hooks to dry underwear and hose.

Since the curtain is usually pulled, the drying garments don't show. If you have a lot of garments on weekends, put one hook between each fold and keep the entire curtain closed. Guests will think you are a neat housekeeper.

One of the greatest time-savers in my kitchen—which also helps keep the kitchen neat—is a plastic container about the shape of a two-pound coffee can. This little "elf" is always sitting on my drainboard just to the right of my sink and it's always over half-full of water. I put all used silverware into it immediately and leave it there until I wash dishes. I never leave a dirty piece of flat silver lying around for a minute.

Not only does this little "helper" soak the silver so that it makes it easy for me to wash when the time comes, but he keeps my drainboard neat and keeps Mr. Disposal from grinding up so many pieces.

A plastic juice container can be used for this. Or if you don't have one, cut off the top of a plastic bleach bottle and use that for a few days to see how you like the idea. Know you'll love it.

And did you know . . . that when you have potato salad, fried eggs, and stuff that usually tarnishes forks, that if you grab that silver real quick and stick it under water, it will not tarnish? Even if you don't clean the table immediately, remember to gather all that flatware and give it to your little "elf" so he can be cleaning it for you.

Never do anything yourself that something else will!

Most of us gals nowadays wear panty hose, but nothing makes me madder than to ruin one stocking and have to throw the whole caboodle away. Some of you have said that you cut off one leg and sew another stocking to it. But that's time, trouble, and usually it doesn't fit.

Just take your scissors and cut off the stocking that has

the run in it. Then when you wear another pair and ruin one leg, cut it off. *Then* put the *two* pairs of the panty hose on at the same time (one left and one right). You'll have a complete new pair again! So what if you've got two pair of thin panties on? That's fine. Some of them are too thin anyway.

I *never* buy just one or two pairs. I buy at least three alike. I keep the tag and next time buy the same brand and color. This can go on for months and months.

Think of the money you are going to save. Why throw something away when it isn't necessary? We all work for those dimes and quarters. And don't forget, odd stockings can be tinted or dyed.

The U.S. Government says, "You can make your own dustcloths that will pick up every bit of dust and will leave a nice shine on the furniture by adding two teaspoons of turpentine to a jar of hot sudsy water, put in a few dustcloths, and screw the lid on tight. Let soak overnight . . .

"All you have to do then is wring out the cloths, hang them up to dry, and they are ready for use. When soiled, they may be washed and reconditioned again. They recommend *old* rags because they are soft and smooth and the lint has worn off."

"Ever wonder where to use spray starch so it doesn't spot everything around the article being treated?

"Lay garments on the wrong side of a rather limp shag rug. When finished, put the rug across the kitchen chair to dry. No more mess and when the ironing is done, you have a well-bodied shag rug to boot!"

"As I was throwing away an old silicon ironing board cover the other day, I noticed one end was still practically new.

"I cut it into small squares and machine-stitched them on one side of every pot holder in my kitchen. I use the silicon side next to my hand when picking up a pot."

"I got tired of dusting the shoes on the floor of my closet, so I finally got smart. I put each pair of shoes in a plastic bread bag and secured the tops with wire 'twistems,' attaching them at the same time to a hanger. Then I just hang them up on the rod in the closet.

"Now there's no need to dust shoes at all and I can easily see which pair I want to wear."

"I always keep a roll of tissue hung over my sink. I find it far less expensive than boxed tissues, takes up absolutely no room, it's out of the way, and it is easy to grab and tear off just as much or as little as one needs.

"I buy the colored tissue to match my decor. This is invaluable for greasing pans, wiping up the spills or crumbs, wiping out ash trays, wiping off grease spatters on the stove, wiping out plates, forks, etc. I also use this for wiping my fingers."

The Latex Foam Rubber Council told us how to keep that foam from coming off the back of our throw and bathroom rugs:

"When washing latex foam-backed rugs, be careful. When the foam is wet, it becomes 'tender' and is apt to tear. Use cold or warm water, *not hot*, and a gentle washing machine agitator speed. Cold water detergents are good. Don't leave the rugs in too long.

"Heat is an enemy of foam rubber. If you have a dryer, use the 'air only' cycle—*no* heat at all because this can dry out the foam rubber. Otherwise, hang the rug where direct sunlight can't reach it. Sunlight is very powerful, and can damage foam rubber seriously in less than an hour.

"Here are a few suggestions:

"If a foam-backed carpet becomes wet, hang it up to dry. Don't leave it in place on the floor, or it might stick.

"Don't use foam-backed carpets outdoors. They are not made for that, and will quickly deteriorate.

"For room-sized rugs, clean with dry suds. Don't saturate the rug.

"Try to keep rugs out of direct sunlight.

"I hope these suggestions will be useful to you and your readers."

"When washing woodwork or the walls, we all know to always start from the bottom and work up, but if you hold a cooky sheet in one hand while using your sponge or rag to wash with the other hand, the pan will catch the spatters from your cloth while washing! This not only saves spatters on the wall but your carpet also."

Another little lollipop friend told me: "An excellent way to mark a dress for hemming on someone not so agile, is to have that person stand at the head of some stairs.

"Then *you* sit on the next lower step."

Folks, while cleaning out my pot and pan cupboard the other day, I happened to notice that I had water rings (caused from hard water) around the inside of a stainless steel pan. And here's what I discovered quite by accident (and I say that so you won't think I'm really smart) . . .

As I had been testing something with rubbing alcohol, I took my alcohol-saturated piece of cotton and wiped around the inside of the pan.

Presto, just as if a little elf had been in there with his magic, all the water rings disappeared! Can you imagine that? Then I tried it on a glass water pitcher and it worked on that, too.

When you bake hot rolls (canned, or boxed, etc.) and only remove half of them to put on your dinner table: Dampen a white paper napkin or towel and lay it over the rolls that remain in the oven. The moisture from the napkin will keep them from becoming too hard until ready to eat.

"That wonderful friend whose suggestion it was to use facial tissue and detergent to wipe mirrors and windows to help keep the moisture off will be forever remembered in my heart. (Just wipe dry without washing off the dab of *liquid* detergent put on with facial tissue.)

"I found after using the facial tissues with the detergent that if I would use a dry paper towel and rewipe the windows, it worked even better.

"The same hint is also good for moisture which collects on storm doors, and the same damp paper towel cleans the metal also. It's terrific! A way to get the windows washed and the storm doors cleaned at the same time."

"To cover nicks and scratches on my dark furniture, I use a little instant coffee. A quarter of a teaspoon or more, depending on the extent of the spot to be covered.

"I mix it with a little water, just enough to make a thick paste, and apply this paste to the scratch mark, rubbing it in well with my finger. I leave a thick layer of the coffee on the mark till it is thoroughly dry. Then with a slightly damp cloth rub off the excess coffee that I left on the unmarked part of the wood.

"You will find that the scar has turned brown and no longer shows. I then wax the spot well with my usual wax. No one will know that the mark was there."

Many working gals complain about picking up the threads off the floor when sewing, especially when patching. I have learned to sew in my kitchen and just sweep up all of those little meanies. Much easier than getting them off the carpet.

Besides, the day I sew is when I do lots of cooking. I'm usually sitting right near the stove and it's convenient to watch the food. And this way I don't burn anything!

But those of you who have cabinet sewing machines that can't be moved to the kitchen, might like to try my method: I take a sheet from my laundry hamper and place it on the floor before I ever start sewing and cutting. Then all I have to do is take the sheet outdoors and shake all of those little threads off when finished! Then dump the sheet back in the hamper.

A plastic shower curtain is even better if you happen to have an old one around. If not, you can buy heavy pieces of plastic at practically any store now for less than fifty cents. You are really not wasting your fifty cents because you'll find you can use this for many, many things thereafter.

"We attached a rubber stair tread to the wooden seat of our little's girl swing. It prevents her from sliding off and from getting splinters. Also, if it rains, the tread can be dried quickly—no more waiting for the wooden seat to dry."

Whenever I buy lemon juice, I get the small can and pour the juice in a clean soy sauce bottle that has the sprinkle top on it. It works just right when anything needs a sprinkling of lemon juice or vinegar.

I find when making buttonholes that if I put iron-on tape

on the wrong side of the material first, it gives body and the material won't fray.

It worked so well for me that I thought others might like to try it.

Lay a piece of foil over an open frying pan to prevent grease from popping out. If it's laid loosely over the pan, the steam can still escape and the food will be crisper.

"At our house, we never use paper napkins for more than one meal, regardless how little they are used. But there is a use for these 'still-good' napkins.

"When we sweep our kitchen floor and must use a dustpan, we dampen one of these napkins and pinch up the little pile of sweepings."

"When you need to carry a flashlight on a rainy or snowy night, just slip it in a plastic bag. This lets the light show through, keeps the flashlight dry, and it can be slipped into pocket or purse when you reach your destination."

"The owner of a candle import shop told me that candles will not drip if the wick is clipped *close* to the candle when lighting. And so far, this has worked for me every time."

Have you ever noticed that when using a box of cake mix how difficult it is to get all the lumps out of it after you have added the liquid?

Well, try beating the mixture before adding the liquid. By beating the dry mixture for a few seconds, you will eliminate all those lumps.

If you have a wide medicine cabinet in the bathroom that has two sliding mirror doors, slide one mirror aside (exposing the shelves) just before running a tub of hot water or taking a hot shower.

When finished bathing, slide the mirror shut. You'll have one clear mirror instead of two steamed, foggy ones.

When sweeping upstairs rooms and you've got a pile of dirt out in the hall, put a newspaper on the first step and sweep the dirt onto it.

That way you won't have extra dirt to sweep down the steps and also you won't have extra dust to breathe.

If you break the lead in your pencil and have no pencil sharpener, try using a potato peeler. Just go about it as if you were peeling a carrot. Works fine.

"If you have a portable sewing machine, take the machine cover off and place it at your feet—upside down. Use it for a thread and scrap catcher.

"It's large enough and hard to miss when placed conveniently. The handle on top (which is now underneath) tips the cover toward you just enough so that it's real handy! Sure saves having to sweep or vacuum the floor each time!"

You know how powder can soil a dark dress around the neck? I use a small piece of wool cut from an old suit. Just rub it over powder smears and it will remove it without a trace.

"When you find drafts coming through vents of window air-conditioners, cover the entire air-conditioner part extending into the room with aluminum foil wrap. Heavy-duty foil works best but regular will do.

"There will be seams but try to avoid too many as the cold air may eventually find its way through. Seal entire seam with adhesive-backed tape. I find it a great improvement, and it doesn't look too bad either."

Mothers of small children have probably learned that when youngsters have their daily bath they usually leave a high-water mark on the tub. So try this: As soon as the water is in the tub, take a bar of soap and run it along the water edge as high as the water will splash! This seems to keep the soil from adhering to the tub and makes it extremely simple to wash the tub afterwards.

And a manufacturer of shirts tells us: "There is absolutely no need to crease the French cuffs on a shirt when it's ironed.

"The French cuff should be ironed out flat and left that way until time to be worn. Then all it needs is a slight crease with your fingers after it's put on.

"By using this method it will keep the soil from grinding into the pressed creases and the shirt will last much longer."

"Want to save a few broken bones?" says one gal with experience.

"I learned the hard way. If you have throw rugs or scatter rugs with a non-skid finish on the backing, please keep this backing *clean!*

"Use a vacuum cleaner, or suds them with a damp sponge once in a while. Remember, these rugs are usually put on highly polished floors and the backing absorbs the wax.

"Every time I sweep, I turn the rug over and sweep the back, plus, I never wax the floor where I leave my throw rugs now."

"I bought a small 'glue-on' towel rack and attached it to the door on the inside of my sewing machine. Now when it stands open, I can hang the various parts of the garment I am stitching on this rod. It is very convenient."

I made a pair of pillowcases from some beautiful pink satin. They're really wonderful. When I toss and turn at night, my hair slides with me and needs very little fixing the next morning.

Next time you're trying to turn a belt after sewing it together . . . instead of using those infernal scissors, go get the biggest screwdriver in the tool chest. It turns that belt like magic without punching holes in it.

I know many of you working gals want to know how to take care of beautiful floors:

First of all, I believe that floors should be dusted daily (either with a dust mop or a vacuum cleaner) so that tracked-in dirt or grit is not ground into the floors. I'm not going so far as to say that you should dust under the couch or bed *every* day. (That's carrying a good thing too far!) I do think the bare areas, where there is the most traffic, should be dusted every day.

And here's a little secret I learned:

If you spray your dust mop with a just a little bit of air freshener, it will dampen the mop so dust and lint will be easy to pick up.

If you use a non-scuff, self-shining wax, the floors should be rewaxed when they become dull.

If you use a type of wax which requires buffing, rewax when the floors no longer shine when you buff them.

Naturally, any spills on the kitchen floor should be wiped up immediately. Use a damp sponge or cloth (wiping with a dry cloth or dry paper towel may leave a dull spot on some waxes) and wipe up the spill gently—don't rub. Then let it dry—don't wipe it dry.

Also, here are two very important cautions on caring for the floors:

Don't ever try to combine leftovers from cans of self-polishing waxes. Different manufacturers use different formulas. Even the same brand changes from time to time as the manufacturers make improvements.

Another thing . . . if you pour wax into a flat container in order to dip an applicator or rag into it, *don't* pour that leftover wax back into its original container. Dirt from the applicator or cloth may be in the leftover wax in the pan, so you won't get the best results with it next time.

### ❦ Bath Towel Blues?

If the edges of your bath towels are fraying—try this: As soon as you see the first fray along the selvages, get out your sewing machine and put it on the biggest and loosest stitch possible—usually it's called a basting stitch. Turn that little edge in and stitch it to the terry cloth part of the towel itself.

Now, what I do is go back and also stitch the outside selvage which I have turned back. This looks like a double stitch on most sport garments. It will last for years and years more.

Also be careful when you buy your next bath towels because manufacturers have written me that some only have a selvage on one side! These bath towels seem to wear only on one side. Have you noticed that?

And here's one of the hottest tips since foil was invented: "Many plastic lids are about the same size and shape but do not fit *every* container even though they look alike.

"So when I bring home any plastic container such as ice cream, cheese, oleo, etc., I immediately write a different number on the top of each lid and the same number on the side of the container that goes with it. Then I know that these two belong together. It's a real time-saver for me, as I don't have to try out each one to see which fits what . . ."

Folks, this is really a top-notch hint, as most of us keep our plastic containers in a dark place such as a pantry corner or under the kitchen cabinet and the lids all piled together in a bowl or a drawer. Use a felt marker because it won't wash off. I found black is the best.

Now, before you ever open a container, give it a number both on top of the lid and around all sides of the container itself in *big* numbers so you can spot them—whether you wear bifocals or not!

Then line those lids up in numerical order. I use 1, 2, 3, etc., and when I get an in-between size, I use 1½, 2½, 3½, etc.

Whenever you're in a tizzy (that means a real hurry), pick up the size container you want, glance at the number on the side, then match it up with the lid that's already marked with the same number. Does it ever save time! No more fumbling around for a matching lid.

Have those of you who like to keep a toothbrush in your purse or make-up kit ever thought of carrying one of those short brushes that are used on electric toothbrushes?

Sure takes up less room and gets the job done just the same. You could even cut off half the handle of a regular toothbrush.

"So many dresses have back zippers now, and I was always snagging my hose when stepping into a dress.

"Then I discovered that if I turn the dress around so that the zipper is in front when I step into it, I can avoid any snags."

"I do a lot of freezing and was using freezer tape like it was going out of style. So I finally thought to use rubber bands instead of tape and they are far superior.

They hold the package tighter and help to get the air out. Best of all, they can be reused.

If any of you working gals have nicotine stains on your fingers: Go to your dime store and buy a little bottle of fingernail *cuticle* remover. Pour some on a cloth or piece of cotton and rub away. Works every time.

If the stains are very heavy and old, it may take one or two applications a day for several days.

For little informal get-togethers, let each one bring his or her frozen dinner or prepared oven dinner. So simple this way. *All* the load is not on any one person, and it lends for more frequent companionship at mealtime.

To apply paste wax to your kitchen floor, simply put a "glob" of the wax inside a folded-down (double thickness) nylon stocking (one with runs, of course) and just rub it on. Works great!

"How can I clean an inexpensive white plastic bag that looks like patent leather? Mine is last year's model and looks awful!"

All I can tell you is how I cleaned my pocketbook. First I used a washcloth and some warm soap suds and got off what I could.

Next I poured some lighter fluid (follow *caution* directions on container—it *is* flammable, you know) on two facial tissues and wiped away. And did it ever clean it! I thought I had a new purse.

About that pinkish stuff on the handle and around the top of the purse . . . the lighter fluid helped remove it but didn't take it all off, so I decided that from now on when I buy an inexpensive, light-colored plastic purse, that I will clean it each month or so with the fluid.

The lighter fluid did not hurt my plastic. I paid three dollars for the purse and figured I had nothing to lose.

"Did you know that aluminum foil may be washed in a dishwasher and used again? Just hang it over the side of the top rack and it comes out like new.

"I held one big piece on the top rack with two clip clothespins."

# Chapter 15

# Some Slick Ideas

If you have ever wrapped up your head at night to preserve a special hairdo, then you know it looks just about as glamorous as bandaging a broken head. Here is a trick that works like magic: Just slide an ordinary nylon slip over your pillowcase at night. You can toss and turn all night and still wake up with a beautiful hairdo.

The nylon slip allows your hair to slide —as you toss and turn—and it doesn't mess up like it will on a cotton pillowcase.

To hold a few slivers of soap together, slip a rubber band (preferably a small one) tightly around the center and allow them to soak a few minutes. Then let dry.

Leave the band on. It doesn't interfere during use, and it holds the small pieces of soap together so they can be used more as hand soap.

### ❦ No Waste Here

Fill your plastic wastebasket with warm soapy water and put your broom in it and slosh it around. Not only does it wash your broom, but it cleans the wastebasket at the same time. Furthermore, you don't even have to stoop to scrub that basket.

### ❦ Revive the Old Pad!

Here's a dilly from another honey pie:

"I found the answer for those who have home floor wax polishers and want to remove the wax from the old pads. Just place the pads between several thicknesses of paper towels and press with a hot iron!

"As you press it, the old wax will melt and absorb into the paper towels. Then you can use the pad again."

### ❦ A Slight Twist

When you store food in a plastic bag that is only half-full (or less), give the bag a few twists and pull the upper unfilled part over the lower filled part. I give it another twist or two and fasten.

Thus there is double protection and a neat package.

And what in the world makes ice cubes stick to the tray and the handle of the insert break when you try to get the ice cubes out?

In the first place, *never* wash your ice trays in hot water or detergents. The trays come from the factory with a coating that prevents sticking, and washing in hot water removes it.

In the second place, don't fill your trays so full of water that when it's frozen, the ice is too near the release gadget on the bottom of the release. That's what breaks them . . .

Now that the coating is evidently off your trays, about

all I can suggest is to buy some spray in a fizz can that says "prevents sticking" and spray your trays with it. It is ordinarily sprayed on skillets and casserole dishes, but will also help to keep ice trays from sticking. It's cheaper than replacing the trays again.

And another of our dear friends says:
"It seems I never have enough closet space. Recently I decided my large walk-in closet could solve that problem. So I had my husband attach a few strong towel racks to the ceiling with long screws.

"Now I hang seldom-used and out-of-season clothes on those ceiling racks. As they are up so high, this leaves plenty of space in the lower half of the closet for other things.

"This beats putting them in boxes and storing them under the bed."

And here's a good one:
"When I make a quantity of iced tea for a picnic, I put it in my insulated jug. I make our tea the strength we like and do not further dilute it with ice cubes.

"So instead of putting the ice cubes loose in the tea, I put them inside a plastic bag, and close it securely with a rubber band. Then I drop the bag and all inside the cooler and let it float in the tea.

"This not only keeps the tea cold without diluting, but we can use the clean ice cubes when we need them.

"This would also be great for other drinks such as lemonade or punch."

Have you ever crawled out of a sickbed to take some medicine, only to face a bottle you couldn't open because of a plastic band around the top?

I have used a paring knife, fork, ice pick, and other sharp objects to pry off the wide plastic band around the top of the bottle, only to wind up with a wounded finger or hand. Suddenly, after years of this, I have found a solution!

Hold the neck of the bottle under your hot water faucet. The band will peel right off, or can be slipped down so that the top can be screwed off.

We have told you about putting a little cologne on your artificial flowers to give them that "for real" scent, but now hear this . . .

For a longer-lasting scent, try putting a bar or two of scented soap in the bottom of the flower container! The scent will last and last, giving the room the wonderful smell of gardenias, roses, old lavender, or whatever fragrance you choose to go with the flowers.

Even the most well-trained dog has "accidents," and here's some good advice: I have been in the laboratories of the National Institute of Rug Cleaning in Washington, D.C. They cope with this problem all the time, and here is their top chemist's answer:

"A dog may be man's best friend, but not necessarily that of man's carpeting. Neglected animal stains have been a problem ever since the 'first accident.'

"Two types of reaction can take place between the chemicals in the urine and those in the fiber dye: Some dyes change color as soon as urine comes in contact with them. Often original color can be restored by immediate addition of a weak solution of ammonia or white vinegar.

"Always pick an inconspicuous area of the carpet and test small amounts of solution to determine its effect on the particular fiber and dye in your own carpet.

"The other change develops slowly over a period of several months and results in permanent change of fiber dye. Not only is there a dye change, but some fibers become weakened or destroyed. After cleaning, these areas are more obvious because the soil which hid the true color has been removed

"The next time your housewives are confronted with an animal 'accident,' I suggest they *immediately* absorb as much liquid as possible.

"Then wash the area with a solution of one teaspoon of neutral detergent (which contains *no bleach*) to one cup of lukewarm water. Absorb all you can with white tissues or toweling.

"Then use a white vinegar solution (one part white vinegar to two parts water) and rewipe the spot.

"Absorb as much as possible.

"Place a half-inch layer of white absorbent material over the area and weigh down with heavy books.

"Allow to dry for at least six hours.

"If *immediate* action is taken to remove these stains in this manner, no change in color should occur and that forgotten 'accident' will not become apparent after your carpet has been *professionally* cleaned."

Bless the National Institute of Rug Cleaners for their compassion in understanding our problems. Aren't they great?

Have you ever tried to open a drawer and found that a box or book had somehow got caught at the very top and defies your frantic efforts to pull out that drawer?

Save your temper and skinned, pinched fingers. Run for your pancake turner. It's just perfect to slide in and force down the stubborn box or article.

So many working gals on a budget complain about tiny

holes appearing in linens that we contacted a laboratory at one of the largest manufacturers of linens. Here is their reply:

"As Director of Homemaking Service for a large manufacturer of household textiles, I answer thousands of letters from homemakers. Many describe "small holes" in sheets. Others complain about changes of color in laundering towels.

"In investigating these complaints, our laboratory usually traces them to careless use of bleach in laundering. As you know, this definitely affects the wear of towels and sheets.

"The problem in using bleach is that women do not take the trouble to read directions. They pour the bleach right into the laundry load. Wherever material touches the bleach, it forms holes. It should be diluted first with water, then poured into the wash water without touching any of the fabric."

I think they were a dreamboat to tell us the cause. I would like to add my two-cents worth about something else I found that causes holes.

Many of us are guilty of using too strong a bleach on our dishcloths, hanging them up to dry, then dumping them in the laundry hamper. Don't do this.

Those cloths might be in the hamper three or four days before you get around to doing your laundry. In the meantime, the bleach from this cloth will get on your nice sheets and clothes. It might damage the fibers. Perhaps you won't see the tiny holes the first time you wash them, but just wait three or four times later. Oh boy!

So always rinse bleached articles thoroughly.

If you iron two of your pillowcases together, then fold them together as one, you'll never lose one of a pair.

Makes a neater looking linen closet, too.

Here is another way to save dollars . . . and everybody has got a faucet!

"As a retired plumber who has made most of his living by replacing washers in dripping faucets, I would like to tip off some of your housewives so they can tell their husbands this little secret.

"Men usually turn off a water faucet too hard. This only wears out the washer because the metal part squeezes and cuts into it.

A faucet should be kept from dripping by turning off gently. Then if it drips, a new washer is definitely needed. But there's absolutely no reason to ruin a washer by squeezing it so hard every time that it gets cut.

"A service call is very expensive. The plumber's time costs the same whether it's to replace a washer or weld a pipe. Also, there is a minimum service charge."

Whenever a serviceman comes to my house, I stand there and watch and see what they do so I might be able to fix it myself next time. What price preventive maintenance? I've saved lots of money this way.

And to save on "whopper" cleaning bills if you have one of those lovely suede coats or jackets which are so fashionable now . . . "I purchased a lovely suede coat, and the manufacturer let me in on their secret method of touch-up cleaning.

"Just rub the mark gently with a gum cleaner eraser and presto . . . the nap of the suede looks like new."

"For small, hard-to-reach spots like painting the inside of a cabinet, try using a plastic squeeze bottle full of paint

*Some Slick Ideas* 243

and dribble it on your brush instead of backing out many, many times to dip that brush in the can.

"If it's a large surface, set a plastic butter tub of the paint inside the work area where it can be reached easily."

"As a manicurist, I wish you would tell the women they should pay their bill before the manicurist puts polish on their fingernails!

"I have seen too many women dig in their purse afterwards and ruin a beautiful manicure by damaging the several coats of polish I put on because they never thought of this before."

If you are in need of extra ice trays, use the new plastic tubs margarine comes in. They will fit into almost any freezing compartment, and the chunk of ice comes out easily after freezing.

And for the absent-minded working "professors" like *me* who get run-down batteries (in your car, not your head, gals) . . .

One sweet thing had these words of caution: "Many people put a tremendous drain on their car batteries, and even run them down to the point of not being able to start their car, by not turning off all the accessories (lights, radio, fan for the heater or air-conditioner) when they park.

"Even though most car ignition switches cut off all the accessories, if these are on when you try to start it, the battery may not be strong enough to turn over the engine with all these things pulling on the battery at the same time.

"I've had this happen to me, so this is the system I set up for myself:

"When I park our car I start counting to six.

"One—I put the gear shift into *park*.

"Two—I set the emergency brake.

"Three—I turn off the radio.

"Four—I turn off the fan, disengage the air-conditioner, or turn off the heater.

"Five—I turn off the ignition and take *out* the key.

"Six—I lock the car.

"If I haven't done six things, I know I've forgotten something.

"All of this only takes about five seconds and it's good insurance that your car will start next time.

"If you don't have all the accessories, you can set up your own counting system. Just be sure to include setting your parking brake and removing the ignition key as a good safety precaution."

It seems that using toweling for play and lounging garments is all the rage now. Really there's nothing like it, especially for stuff to wear around the house but . . . it does shrink.

I bought a terry cloth robe, which was one of the best brands, in my regular size. But I soon learned that I should have bought two sizes larger. You know why? Because the sleeves in that robe shrunk two inches when I sent it to be laundered.

If we wash these robes at home or take them to a laundromat, they don't shrink as much as when we send them out to a laundry. But don't blame the laundry for this.

The reason our clothes get whiter when sent to a laundry is because their water is hotter than ours!

So all I can say is to get a bigger size when you buy anything made out of terry cloth or toweling. And if you make your own garments out of toweling, allow for that shrinkage.

And, dear folks, before laying your own wall-to-wall carpets, especially runners on stairways, halls, and bathrooms —test which way the nap runs!

All you have to do is take a broom or your hand and sweep or rub the carpeting gently. The direction the nap runs will show immediately. It will rub or sweep hard one way and easy another. The rug will also shade just a little.

Don't lay the rug with the nap running the wrong way.

*Always lay carpets with the nap running the direction in which you ordinarily sweep.*

In your hall, on a stairway, or in the living room or bedroom, always lay it with the nap running toward the door . . . or down a staircase or toward the entrance where you collect the dust in a long hall.

This not only prevents imbedded dust in your carpet, but it is far easier to clean it. Sure saves energy and your carpet in the long run.

If you like to read a good book in bed (and this is especially good for those who are sick), try putting a pillow or facial tissue box on your stomach and your book on top of that! Takes all the strain off your arms and shoulders.

When I'm sitting up, I put a pillow in my lap and rest the book on it while reading.

Did you know that if you spray your bra straps with starch they won't roll or twist? They lay flat against your skin like new!

Here's another wonderful idea for those who have electric fry pans that eventually wear out, and either cannot be repaired, or it's cheaper to buy a new one . . . Don't throw them away!

Using a screwdriver, I removed the legs and now have

a wonderful heavy skillet to use over my burners! I am so proud now to use it for long-cooking food while we have a new electric skillet for something else.

Has anyone ever suggested that you can use nail polish to mark the family toothbrushes?

The polish stays on the handles and does not interfere with the use of the brush.

Dots or lines can be used in any sort of code . . . one dot for the smallest child, two for the next, etc., or lines for the grown-ups.

I find this quite handy.

Pure lemon extract will remove the ink-stamped prices on products. Use it straight as it comes from the bottle.

## Closing

And now our little book is drawing to a close, so I'll just say, "Good-bye for now and may God bless you all . . . I love you dearly."

Forever yours,
Heloise

# ꙍ Index

*Index*   257

Rugs, *see* Carpets; Foam-backed rugs;
Shag rugs; Throw rugs

Safety, *see* Highway safety; Home
safety
Salad dressing
from leftover dip, 161
for potato salad, 168–69
for tossed salad, 170
Salad preparation, 158–60
colorful salads, 107–8
coring lettuce in, 158
egg salad, 102–3, 159, 161
ham salad, 203
for lunch at office, 124
pickled beans for, 171–72
potato salad, 159, 168–69, 193
preventing salad wilting, 158
tuna-fish salad, 160
*See also* Cole slaw
Salads
kept cool for picnics, 159
storage of, 127
Salisbury steak, 194
Salmon croquettes, 207
Salt, cure for damp, 170–71
Sandboxes, indoor-outdoor, 38–39
Sandwich preparation, 157–58
bean sandwiches, 189–90
egg-salad sandwiches, 102–3, 126
fancy sandwiches, 157–58
meat-loaf sandwiches, 193
packing lunch sandwiches, 126–27,
157
pickles for, 207
thin-sliced bread for, 125–26
tuna-fish sandwiches, 160
*See also* Hamburgers
Scarves, preventing loss of, 85
Scatter rugs, *see* Shag rugs; Throw
rugs
Schappert, Edna, 90, 92–93
School and home training, 39
Screens, dusty, 136
"Seasoning" laundry, 16
Sewing, 17–21, 100
adding pockets, 20
alterations, 19, 21
belts, 232
buttonholing, 228–29
of café curtains, 115
dust ruffles, 35
hems, 226
lingerie, 92
litter from, 228, 230

machine, 6, 211, 228, 230, 232
nappy fabrics, 18
pinning, 97
snaps instead of hooks and eyes, 21
terry cloth, 245
Sewing baskets, 108
Shag rugs, 113, 224
Shelf linings, 61–62
Shoe care
dust-free storage, 225
polishing, 37, 151–52, 154
prevention of scuffing, 149
"rest" period, 149
for rubber sandals, 152
Shoes, 149–52
baby, 37
breaking in new, 149–50
elastic laces, 217
marked for easy dressing, 38, 217–
18
storing, 225
Shower curtains
laundering, 145, 220
remove mildew from, 145
Shower caps, 50
Silver platters, 219
Sinks, 134–35
Sleep
baby's, 34–35, 67
hairdo protection during, 232, 237
sleeping in curlers, 47
using periods of insomnia, 211–12
*See also* Beds
Slip straps, hiding, 92
Slipcovers, *see* Upholstery
Soap sliver bundle, 237
Soil prevention, 94
for carpets, 30, 246
for French cuffs, 231
ink-stain prevention, 219
preventing collar lines, 11
starching as, 16
for synthetics, 7
tarnish prevention, 223
for upholstered furniture, 100
for white cotton gloves, 14
for white dresses, 94
*See also* Stain removal
Sorting
costume jewelry, 87
items for charity, 22
Space saving
closet space, 17, 239
in cupboard, 173
at table, 32

258    *Index*

*Index*   259

Toothbrushes, 235, 247
Toys, *see* Children's toys
Trading stamp books, filling, 212
Travel
    with children, 33
    home movies of, 78
    wrinkle-free packing for, 96–97
Tricycle seat covers, 110
Turkey
    foil-covered legs, 202
    foil-covered platters, 218–19
    greased foil for roasting, 204
    purchasing and storing, 200

Uniforms
    reinforcement of, 84
    white, 93
Upholstery
    automobile, remedying hot, 121
    cleaning, 100
    removing and replacing cushion
        covers, 215
    repairing slipcovers for, 143
    slipcover material protecting, 113

Vacations, home movies of, 78
Vacuum cleaners, 135–36
Vitamins administered to babies, 41

Waffles
    folding eggs into, 197
    leftover, 112
    melting oleo for, 209
Walnut furniture, cleaning, 141
Warming breads in foil, 209
Wash-and-wear garments, *see* Drip-
    dry garments
Washing machines, 7–8

suds overflow in, 100
Waste baskets, 116, 238
Wax removal, 104, 140, 238
Waxing
    applying paste wax, 235–36
    beneath throw rugs, 232
    overwaxing furniture, 141
    rewaxing, 233
Weeding, 76
Wieners
    biscuit-wrapped, 192
    chili dogs, 207–8
    potatoes and leftover, 187–88
Wig stand, 47
Windowsill liners, 62, 65
Windows, 59–61
    carbon on, 139
    frosting, 59–60
    removing moisture from, 227
    sealing, 61, 62–63, 231
    tips for decorating, 60–61, 65, 110,
        112
    washing, 82, 227
Windowscreens, 136
Wire baskets
    popcorn kernels shaken from, 206
    vegetables boiled in, 201–2
Woodwork
    cleaner test for painted, 136–37
    painting baseboards, 64
    washing, 79–80, 226
Woolens, 220
    cure for rump-sprung knits, 85
    pressing pleated skirts, 15
    sewing with, 18
    *See also* Sweaters

Zippers, remedy for stubborn metal,
    83